WITHDRAWN

# The Divine Narcissus
## *El Divino Narciso*

Portrait of Juana Inés de la Cruz (Copy of Self Portrait)
Unknown Mexican artist, 18th century, 41 1/2" x 31",
oil on canvas, No. '03-918
Courtesy Philadelphia Museum of Art:
The Dr. Robert H. Lamborn Collection

# The Divine Narcissus
## *El Divino Narciso*

*by Sor Juana Inés de la Cruz*

TRANSLATED AND ANNOTATED BY
Patricia A. Peters
and Renée Domeier, O.S.B.

ALBUQUERQUE, UNIVERSITY OF NEW MEXICO PRESS

1998 by the University of New Mexico Press. Spanish text of
*El Divino Narciso* reprinted, annotated, and modified by permission
of the publisher from *Obras Completas de Sor Juana Inés de la Cruz*,
vol. 3, Alfonso Méndez Plancarte, editor, copyright 1951
Fondo de Cultura Económica.
First edition

Library of Congress Cataloging-in-Publication Data
Juana Inés de la Cruz, Sister, 1651–1695.
[Divino Narciso, English & Spanish]
The Divine Narcissus—El divino Narciso / by Sor Juana Inés de la Cruz;
translated and annotated by Patricia A. Peters and Renée Domeier.—1st ed.
p.    cm. Includes bibliographical references and index.
ISBN 0-8263-1930-0 (cloth), ISBN 0-8263-1888-6 (pbk.)
1. Narcissus (Greek mythology)—Drama.
2. Echo (Greek mythology)–Drama.
I. Peters, Patricia A., 1935–   .
II. Domeier, Renée, 1933–   .
III. Title.
PQ7296.J6D5813  1988
862—dc21
97–37546
CIP

*To the women in my family who have challenged, inspired, and loved me: my grandmother Elizabeth, who gave me my cultural heritage baked into countless strudels and in old country stories of as many layers; my mother Rosalie, whose motto, "Try everything and you'll find something you love," has guided my life; my sister Liz, who shares my heart and faith; my Aunt Johanna, a "Juana" who stimulates my mind and eases it with her good sense; my daughters Mary Rose and Cat and my daughter-in-law Sue, who have supported me in good times and bad and cook up wonderful fun at all times; and my wondrous granddaughters, Elizabeth Alexis and Emily Patricia, who fill my days with joy and my spirit with hope*
*—Patricia A. Peters*

*To my Hispanic brothers and sisters who have opened up a whole new world to me*
*—Renée Domeier, O.S.B.*

# Contents

# Introduction

PATRICIA A. PETERS

## The Author

Sor (Sister) Juana Inés de la Cruz (1648/51?–1695), canonized by literary historians of Spain's Golden Age, but not by the church she served, is considered the last great practitioner in Spanish poetry of the baroque style, which dominated European literature, music, architecture, painting, and sculpture in the seventeenth century. Essentially theatrical, baroque art, like the geographic colonization of that age, ignores boundaries, and it escapes the borders of both genre and medium. Paintings like those of El Greco, for example, often refuse to limit their spatial domain to the dimensions of their frames while Bernini's sculpture of St. Teresa of Avila is placed in a stagelike setting with theater boxes on either side of the sculpture. Baroque poetry ignores boundaries too. It stretches rhetoric beyond conventional limits and abounds in conceits that find correspondences between concepts that inhabit different intellectual worlds. Opera, written in many languages, with its sung conversations, monumental choruses, characters of many races and classes, and spectacular stage effects, was born in a baroque crosscultural marriage between drama and music and nursed by the visual arts.

Sor Juana was, paradoxically, equally at home in the international world of the baroque and in the cloistered convent of Santa Paula of the Order of San Jerónimo in Mexico City, where she lived most of her life. Like the frame of a baroque painting, the cloister walls could not contain the artistic and intellectual space of the beautiful, multitalented nun. Her letters, lyrics, drama, and liturgical writings went out from her cell-study, and they drew into the convent parlor representatives of both the viceregal court and the Roman Catholic clergy, the two powerful forces on which the Spanish Empire in America was built. For nearly twenty-five years, Sor Juana's deft diplomacy, talent, intelligence, and wit kept her in fruitful relationship with those formidable patriarchal institutions, the court and the church, benefiting her convent and assuring herself time and space to study and write while she faithfully carried out her duties in the community and the prayer life demanded by *The*

*Rule of Saint Augustine,* the cornerstone of spiritual formation for the Sisters of San Jerónimo. Saint Augustine, one of the early Fathers of the Church, had written a rule characterized by brevity, sensitivity to the varying capacities for rigor of those from different classes and conditions, and considerable attention to both the value and difficulties of living in community. For Sor Juana, the Augustinian rule provided parameters and protection under which she could live out her calling as a Sister, scholar, and artist.

Earlier, in 1666, Juana de Asbaje y Ramírez de Santillana had attempted for three months to live the far stricter Carmelite rule in the Convent of San José, but she returned to the court, where renowned for her learning and beauty, she had been a lady-in-waiting to the vicereine. Probably, the severity of the Carmelite lifestyle after the comforts of the court had broken her health. "Indeed, in the late eighteenth century a commentator had to say about the Carmelites of St. Teresa that 'there were few, in spite of their strength, who did not become sick a few days after professing, and two-thirds of the community (at least) were constantly ill in the infirmary'" (Lavrin, "Values and Meaning of Monastic Life" 375). There is no evidence that the Carmelites had been much less rigorous during the preceding century. Undoubtedly, Juana was only one among many to leave the Carmelites before profession.

Unable to survive the test of penitential rigor, Juana next faced a traditional test for scholarship. To publicly prove her wide range of knowledge, thought impossible for a woman, the viceregent gathered forty experts in various fields for a public oral examination of her. She distinguished herself as an autodidact whose educational institution had been her grandfather's library, the only tutor available to a young female scholar of her social class. The adulation her performance inspired alarmed her Jesuit confessor, Antonio Núñez de Miranda. In 1669, with his insistent help, she entered the more moderate convent of Santa Paula, where she made her vows and took the name of Sor Juana Inés de la Cruz. There, despite petty jealousies and ecclesiastical pressures to live a more conventionally holy life, she enjoyed a quarter century of intellectual activity and literary productivity until she inadvertently wandered into a minefield of theological debate.

In November 1690, without her permission, Bishop Manuel Fernández de Santa Cruz published a manuscript by Sor Juana, which he titled *Carta atenagórica* (*Letter Worthy of Athena*). In it, she had set to paper her critique of a sermon delivered forty years before by the Jesuit Antonio Vieyra, who claimed to refute several church Fathers, among them Saint Augustine, author of the rule by which she and her Sisters lived. With a copy of her *Letter* the bishop sent her his response, written under the pseudonym of Sor Filotea de la Cruz, in which he advised her to study Sacred Scripture rather than humane letters. After three months, she responded with her famous *La Respuesta* (*The Answer*), which was not published until after her death. In it, Sor Juana argues that humane letters are a necessary preparation and complement for understanding Scripture, not an obstacle, an idea that she had already incorporated into *The Divine Narcissus* two or three years before (*auto* ll.125–30). *The Answer* contains, in addition, her intellectual autobiography. In it, she defends herself as a poet, citing the undoubted value of poetry in the Bible, especially that of David in the psalms and Solomon's *Canticle of Canticles*, both of which she draws on heavily in *The Divine Narcissus*. Her apologia for her intellectual life expands into a brilliant defense of the rights of women to education and written expression, for which she has frequently been named the first feminist in America.

Both as a defender of women's rights and as a lyric poet, Sor Juana has been widely anthologized in Spanish and English. In his monumental biography, Octavio Paz names her as one of five women whom he ranks among the major poets of our hemisphere (*Sor Juana, or The Traps of Faith* 1). Although *The Divine Narcissus* is one of the finest extant examples of the *auto sacramental*, the popular drama that celebrated the feast of Corpus Christi, her religious works have not been so widely anthologized and translated as *The Answer* and her secular lyric poetry. Artistically far superior to the English *Everyman*, it has never received the same critical attention. What is worse, the practice of reading Sor Juana chiefly through *The Answer* and her secular poetry has led to her acknowledgment as a poet, an intellectual, and a defender of women's rights, but it has made possible the denigration of her vocation as a nun who prays, reads, thinks, and writes—all as part of her religious calling. *The Divine Narcissus* reveals Sor Juana the nun and artist who creates out of felt liturgical experiences as well as literary precedents and a biographical crisis.

Most of what we know about the life of Sor Juana is derived from the autobiographical portions of *The Answer* and a biography by her contemporary, Father Diego Calleja, who corresponded with Sor Juana and wrote the preface to a posthumous edition of her works. His biography contains the account of the oral examination at court. In *The Answer*, Sor Juana focuses only on her intellectual development from childhood through the convent years and her life as a member of the religious community and the Catholic church. What is left out is significant: details of her family life, especially that her mother was an unmarried, independent, able, unlettered Mexican woman; her life at court, including the oral examination; and her time in the Carmelite convent. A baptismal certificate, an eighteenth-century copy of a letter dismissing her confessor, convent documents, her mother's will, and a great deal of speculation fill in the missing information.

Even the birth date given by Calleja, 1648, has been called into question by the 1651 baptismal certificate from Chimalhuacán, which makes clear the illegitimacy of the baby named Inés, whose sponsors, like Sor Juana's mother Isabel, were named Ramírez. This document and her mother's last will, which testifies that her children were born out of wedlock, are often cited as evidence that Sor Juana's decision to enter the convent was inspired to some extent by her illegitimacy, which rendered her a poor candidate for a suitable marriage proposal. However, the same social code applied to the convent, and Sor Juana signed her profession as the legal daughter of Pedro de Asbaje. There is really no evidence that she lied. Since, as Asunción Lavrin points out, until shortly before her death, Isabel Ramírez, Sor Juana's mother, described herself as the widow of Pedro de Asbaje, Sor Juana may not have known when she entered the convent that her parents had not been married ("Sor Juana, Nuns and Nunneries in Baroque Mexico" 6).

Another frequently offered explanation why Sor Juana chose the convent rather than marriage is her alleged lack of the requisite bridal dowry. Economically also, the requirements of convent and courtship were comparable. "The endowment of a nun ranged from 2,000 to 4,000 pesos in the XVII and XVIII centuries . . . [while] doweries of most brides were roughly between 1,000 and 5,000 pesos" (Lavrin, "Unlike Sor Juana" 75).

Why did Juana Ramírez enter the convent then? In *La Respuesta*, Sor Juana answers that question at length:

> I took the veil because, although I knew I would find in
> religious life many things that would be quite opposed to my
> character (I speak of accessory rather than essential matters), it
> would, given my absolute unwillingness to enter into mar-
> riage, be the least unfitting and the most decent state I could
> choose, with regard to the assurance I desired of my salvation.
> For before this first concern (which is, at the last, the most
> important), all the impertinent little follies of my character
> gave way and bowed to the yoke. These were wanting to live
> alone and not wanting to have either obligations that would

disturb my freedom to study or the noise of a community that would interrupt the tranquil silence of my books. These things made me waver somewhat in my decision until, becoming enlightened by learned people as to my temptation, I vanquished it with divine favor and took the state I so unworthily hold. I thought I was fleeing myself, but—woe is me!—I brought myself with me, and brought my greatest enemy in my inclination to study, which I know not whether to take as a Heaven-sent favor or as a punishment. (trans. Arenal and Powell 51)

Here is the voice, not of a starry-eyed novice, but of a mature and rational woman, analyzing her earlier motives after twenty years as a Sister. Marriage is a sacrament, but not one she desired. Since marriages of women of her social class were arranged by others and childbirth was frequent and dangerous, Juana and her contemporaries had few romantic illusions about the married state, and she was not alone in her "absolute unwillingness." Only one choice remained that assured her of attaining her primary goal, her salvation. But wanting to be alone to study and having no illusions about the noise and demands of community life, she didn't find the convent very attractive either. Only with spiritual direction did she "bow to the yoke" and attempt to leave her wayward ego behind. With humorous chagrin, she admits that it managed to creep in too, along with her insatiable need to study, which she doesn't know if she should name a curse or a blessing. And no wonder! It is Sor Juana's call as a scholar and writer, not her antipathy to marriage and hesitation about convent life, that sets her apart from most other nuns of the medieval and early modern periods. Despite the popular notion that the decision to take vows in religion grew from a girl's desire to be united to Jesus, many who entered convents did so hoping for both protection from undesirable marriages and a measure of autonomy in a world controlled by men. More than a few entered communities reluctantly. Among them was St. Teresa of Avila, whose autobiography is the contemporary prototype.

There are parallels in the two autobiographical accounts. Like Sor Juana, Santa Teresa feared marriage (*Life* 74), had difficulty in finding a suitable confessor (113), and described herself as the weakest and most wicked sinner (108). Teresa was also commanded by her religious superiors to write. The anxiety of conflicting demands, much like those which Sor Juana details in *The Answer*, surface in St. Teresa's *Life* as well:

I am stealing the time for writing, and that with great difficulty, for it hinders me from spinning, and I am living in a
poor house and have numerous things to do. (123)

Similarly, Sor Juana:

I had interruptions, posed not only by my religious duties (for
it is well known how usefully and beneficially these take up
one's time), but by all those other things incidental to life in a
community. (59)

One great difference outweighs these similarities. St. Teresa's autobiography has as its purpose the description of mystical prayer.
Sor Juana's is an apologia for her own religious vocation expressed
chiefly as a scholar and artist. Her portraits show her against a
background of books, with a pen in her hand, consciously meeting
the eye of the viewer. The most famous depiction of St. Teresa is
Bernini's swooning, semiconscious ecstatic, pierced by the darts of
a baroque cherub who looks more like Cupid than Gabriel. Like
much mystical art, the sculpture speaks with the erotic diction of
*The Canticle of Canticles* and the secular love lyric, a language Sor
Juana employed herself in her secular poetry and in *The Divine
Narcissus*. That she rejected that diction for recounting her life as a
nun makes her construction of her religious life congruent with
only part of the contemporary cultural model. Her verbal self-portrait lacks the erotic piety and passivity conventionally expected of
nuns in the seventeenth century.

Admittedly, Bernini's baroque St. Teresa has as its source a passage from her *Life*, in which she describes mystical prayer. Unfortunately, that image is seldom balanced with the rest of her often
earthy, practical writing. Ritamary Bradley points out that in her
exegesis of *The Canticle of Canticles* (hidden by her community
for fear of the Inquisition), St. Teresa "conflates the images of
spouse, friend, teacher, and mother (128). The emphasis on the spou-
sal metaphor grows out of a male tradition based on, Bradley says,
"the notion that a woman, inferior in intellect and the vessel of
lust, is capable of no other approach to God than a slight glossing
of natural instincts directed toward Jesus, the man" (152). In fact,
up to and including the first half of the twentieth century, most
ceremonies celebrating women's receiving the habit have begun
with the candidates approaching the altar clothed as brides—the
brides of Christ. In contrast, no male monastic has ever been made
to present himself in chapel dressed as a bridegroom of the church
before receiving the habit of his order.

Measured by the prevailing cultural bridal metaphor, then, Sor Juana has been found wanting as a nun by many of her male critics such as Ermilo Abreu Gómez, editor of the first critical editions of her works, who wrote in 1934 in a long prologue that hers was a fake vocation by which she deceived others to satisfy her own intellectual needs. Thirty years later, she was posthumously analyzed by Ludwig Pfandl, who saw her devotion to books as a sexual aberration and accused her of penis envy and menopausal neurosis. In 1953, the poet Robert Graves wrote of her "oddness" with more sympathy, but concluded that she lacked "sufficient resolution either to stick it out as a muse or make a complete [religious] abnegation" (9). Most recently, her biographer Octavio Paz, after claiming her as one of Mexico's greatest poets, found her guilty of narcissism, devoid of a religious calling, and in the habit of unhealthy sexual sublimation: "Convent and library are compensation for the stepfather and substitute for the father. And they fill the same emotional need, since cell and library are rooted in the same soil as infantile desire" (79). Paz agrees that Sor Juana had no authentic vocation and offers as proof Calleja's remark that "twenty-seven years she lived the life of a nun without the seclusion that earns ecstatics their glory and good name, but substantially fulfilling her religious obligations" (105).

These men's implied definitions of vocation resonate with centuries of cultural overlay, defining "the call from God" for a woman as a mysterious disembodied voice, courting her into a self-abnegating life-style based on the erotic image of a young bride whose ego-boundaries are blurred into identity with her spouse. Since a strong ego is essential for a woman scholar-artist, such self-abnegation would not permit Sor Juana to use her abilities in the manner she believed we all are obligated to make use "of the talents He bestowed on us, and of the gifts He lent us, for which we must one day render Him a most detailed account" (*The Answer/La Respuesta* 101). Father Antonio Núñez, Sor Juana's confessor, did not agree. In his *Distribución de las obras ordinarias*, he asserts that the nun should "cut the adornments of talent with the knife of mortification" (Lavrin, "Unlike Sor Juana" 86). For Sor Juana, talent was not an adornment but part of her call, and evidently her superiors usually agreed with her, for she mentions only one occasion at San Jerónimo when she was ordered not to study and asserts that she was commanded to write. Despite popular contemporary male fantasies about a nun's vocation, she saw her calling as faithfully following the rule of her order and using her talents to the best of her ability, despite the inconveniences of community life. Today, few Sisters would disagree with her definition of a religious vocation. Even female literary critics, however, respond to her identity as a nun very differently from women who live the same vows as Sor Juana's.

Modern feminist critics pursue quite different political agenda from those of the men. Most justifiably write of Sor Juana as a martyr of the patriarchy that limited her marriage choices, attempted to control her intellectual and artistic choices, and eventually silenced her when her choices were no longer congruent with the gender roles dictated by her church and culture. Focused on *The Answer*, these critics read Sor Juana's religious life in the church as chiefly adversarial and rather static. Relatively few consider her as a Sister who experienced spiritual growth as well as intellectual development over her twenty-five years of living the community rule. The thin line between autobiography and fiction becomes invisible in some feminist artistic treatments of Sor Juana. Diane Ackerman's beautiful dramatic poem, *Reverse Thunder*, is a case in point. It imagines "Juana" meeting a young Italian ambassador outside the convent and consummating a passionate love. The lover dies at sea, and this knowledge along with the penances imposed by the bishop of Puebla for her writing weakens Sor Juana, who succumbs to the plague.

While not all cloistered nuns were celibate, a highly visible and politically besieged cloistered scholar and writer in seventeenth-century Mexico would have to be both foolhardy and possessed of many cooperative friends to manage such an affair. *The Answer* lacks any hint that Sor Juana might have had the folly or the friends to effect a tryst. It is, perhaps, the admiration and love of twentieth-century feminist writers which tempts them to cast her in roles that the twentieth century values, but which she could never have played. What evidence we have makes it clear that her life was more than full with her duties as convent treasurer, her letter-writing, scholarship, and significantly large literary output as well as her attendance at community prayers for the canonical Hours. There is no evidence that she ever left the confines of San Jerónimo after the gates closed behind her as a candidate, not even to assist in the civic and liturgical celebrations for which she sent designs, poetry, and music, or to direct or watch a play of her own making.

Having lived according to her own conscience and having defended her vocation as a woman who thinks, reads, and writes as well as one who prays, Sor Juana saw in her final years doors closing on her vocation as a scholar and writer. In 1689, the viceregency changed to governors less friendly and protective toward Sor Juana than the previous officials had been. Bad weather resulting in poor crops and the civil unrest that accompanies famine occupied their attention. With the publication of her works, especially *The Letter*, ecclesiastical pressures for her to abandon secular studies and writing increased. After writing *The Answer*, she continued to work for two more years. Perhaps the year of preparation for her silver jubilee, the twenty-fifth anniversary of her entrance into religious life, occasioned her radical change of direction. In 1693, she sold her books and instruments, signed the customary general confession, and focused on the parts of her vocation still open to her, her prayer life and relationships within the community. In 1695, while nursing her sick Sisters of the convent during an outbreak of the plague, she contracted the illness and died as she had lived, faithfully keeping the rule and, with practical wisdom, using her gifts as well as possible.

Feminist writers have made much of the phrasing of her general confession, "I, the worst of all." In fact, a recent film about her takes its title from this conventional formula, also used by St. Teresa and many other nuns in the early modern period. Neither this confession (which may have only been signed by Sor Juana, but not composed by her,) nor any other document, least of all, her dramas, sheds much light on Sor Juana's personal emotional states. Unlike many of her contemporaries, she shared her intellect, but kept her inner life private. What *The Divine Narcissus* does do is show us her familiarity with Scripture, not simply as a scholar, but as a Sister whose liturgical life in chapel and understanding of doctrine are carried to her writing desk and transformed into a lovely pastoral drama of redemption, framed by a remarkable reflection on the plight of the Aztecs under the scourge of Spanish colonization.

## The Play

### 1. Genre, Composition, and Early Editions

*The Divine Narcissus* is an *auto sacramental*, that is, a rather long one-act play honoring the Holy Eucharist and usually performed on the feast of Corpus Christi (The Body of Christ), the Thursday after Trinity Sunday, which occurs in late May or early June. A form of popular drama written by some of the best Spanish authors and acted by professionals in the streets and sometimes at court as well, the *auto* flourished from the late fifteenth century to the early eighteenth century. As seems to be true of English mystery plays, *autos* were mounted on *carros*, which could be moved from one place to another. Each play required several carts, one of which was used as a center stage and was flanked by others. Sometimes two-storied, the flanking *carros* provided settings, storage of stage properties, and a place for actors to change costume, enter and exit. For his *autos*, Calderón de la Barca, the undisputed master of the form in the seventeenth century, was known to use as many as eight carts, including the center stage (McKendrick 248–49).

Allegorical in content, these plays were required to relate thematically to the mystery of the Holy Eucharist and to provide theological instruction, especially during the Counter-Reformation. Their broad audience included common laborers, royalty, and clergy. Typically baroque in their combinations of the arts, *autos* presented poetry, instrumental and choral music, dance, and spectacular effects blended to cause delight, awe, and religious fervor in the spectator, at least during the duration of the performance, if not longer. In New Spain, some of the ingredients were gathered from the various traditions of the multicultural population as well as from Scripture and classical sources.

Sor Juana came to the *auto* already experienced in writing for a popular audience as well as for court and convent. She had published many examples of the *villancico*, "(from *villano*, peasant): originally a poem in short lines in the manner of the songs sung by peasants; in Sor Juana's time, one of a sequence of lyrics composed to be sung at matins [the early morning service], on a religious holiday" (Paz 514). As a *criolla* whose father was probably from Spain and whose mother had been born in Mexico, she had access to Spanish, Black dialect, and Nahuatl, the language of the Indians, all of which appear in her *villancicos*. In the *loa* of *The Divine Narcissus*, she draws as well on her knowledge of popular culture, probably gained from childhood experience as well as from reading. Her mother managed her grandfather's ranch, and documentary evidence shows that she bought slaves, and later gave one, a twelve-year-old mulatto, Juana de San José, to her daughter when she entered the convent (Tavard 5) and whom Sor Juana later freed. Since the use of slaves and servants in convents was common, there the population was just as multiracial as on a ranch or in the city and just as socially hierarchical:

at the top, nuns of the black veil, fully doweried, supposedly legitimate of birth and pure of blood; in the middle, *mestizo* and Indian servants; and at the bottom mulatto and black slaves, some belonging to the community at large, some to individual nuns. (Arenal, "Aria of a Cloistered Feminist" 50)

Yet when the black-veiled Sor Juana creates the Aztec America in *The Divine Narcissus*, she gives her speeches with a dignity and beauty surpassing those of the Spanish pure-blooded Religion—a radical reversal of contemporary social hierarchical values.

Sor Juana composed *The Divine Narcissus* and its *loa* around 1688. According to some sources, she wrote it at the request of her friend and patroness Vicereine María Luisa de Laguna, countess of Paredes, who took it with her to Spain when she returned after eight years in Mexico, the first six of which she and her husband had presided over the court and governed the Spanish colony. According to the title page of the first edition, published in Mexico in 1690, María Luisa took the play to Madrid in 1689, not for publication in the first collection of Sor Juana's works, *Castilian Inundation*, but for presentation there that year.

For over thirty years before his death in 1681 and for several years afterward, Calderón de la Barca had dominated the Corpus Christi festivals in Madrid with his *autos*. Only in 1687 was the competition opened to new authors. Such an innovation must have encouraged Sor Juana to write her *auto* despite her residence in New Spain, and indeed, at the end of the *loa*, Religion announces that she will write a play called *The Divine Narcissus* to be presented in the crown city. Zeal argues that it is not proper that something should be written in the colony for presentation in Madrid. Perhaps Zeal expresses Spanish official opinion, for two of Calderón's *autos* were in rehearsal for the 1689 festival, which was canceled because of the death of the queen (McKendrick 259). There is no record that Sor Juana's play was ever acted in her lifetime.

After its publication in a separate edition in 1690, *The Divine Narcissus* appeared in volume 2 of her *Obras* in 1692, which was printed in five separate editions. The play appeared again in five more editions, which included volume 3, in 1700. In 1725 the three volumes were printed once more, the last edition before the late nineteenth century. The present edition uses the standard critical text in volume 3 of *Obras Completas*, edited and annotated by Alfonso Méndez Plancarte in 1955.

## 2. *The* Loa

Developed in the sixteenth century in Spain, the *loa* is usually a preface to a comedy or religious play, which introduces the themes of the longer play, often through humorous dialogue. Thus, its purpose is much like that of the induction of English plays in approximately the same period.

Sor Juana's interest in writing about the Eucharist, the subject of *The Divine Narcissus,* goes back to her childhood. Her first known composition is a *loa* to the Blessed Sacrament, which she wrote in 1658. The seriousness of the themes in the *loa* of *The Divine Narcissus*—religious doctrine, colonization, with its accompanying repression of native peoples and damage to the environment, and salvation—is tempered by humor. This later *loa* is comic in its subtle attacks on conventional expectations about gender.

On the surface, the structure suggests a debate in which the sides are evenly balanced in terms of gender. Zeal, the *conquistador,* and Religion, the Spanish lady, debate the nature of the true God with the Aztec prince and princess, Occident and America. Yet the two women carry the arguments. America defends Aztec worship of the sun god in human sacrifice and the sharing of the seed-and-blood idol in a ritual meal. Religion counters that Aztec ceremonies are a diabolic imitation of the Holy Eucharist and insists that the Aztecs convert. Zeal is revealed as an overzealous war horse, who persuades by force and chafes at the bit to introduce his guns into the argument, but he follows Religion's orders and gives only weak opposition to her ideas. Occident has more dignity but much naiveté. Sometimes, he merely echoes what America says; at others, he stands back and listens to America argue. At one point, she gives him and his cohorts direct orders. Both male characters parody *machismo.* In the seventeenth century, with their eloquent claims to liberty and author-ity, both women characters must have seemed *varonil,* much as Sor Juana is described by Pfandl. To the extent that Religion represents "Mother Church," dominated completely by power-wielding masculine mores that keep female religious in enclosure, Religion fits the type rather well, especially at the beginning of the *loa.* Her creator, Sor Juana, of course, writes from an enclosed space provided by Religion, supposedly a room of her own, to which Religion holds the key. Her conflicted response is eloquently described by Irving Leonard in his valuable study, *Baroque Times in Old Mexico:*

The love and kindliness implicit in the Church's paternalism claimed her gratitude and, of course, her vows compelled obedience to it. Yet the persistent longing for a freer expression of her intuition and for another and more open avenue to truth and to God prevented complete reciprocation and submission in her heart. The sensate experimentalism and scientific methodology of a dawning age beckoned her. (188)

The female characters of the *loa* allegorize the conflict. In Religion there is both high poetry and considerable self-deception. She portrays herself as compassionate, but actually controls Zeal's use of horses and firearms against the awestruck Indians. Eventually, she better mirrors her own positive self-image. Even an allegorical character can develop, and within her short play, Religion does move toward more attractive human qualities from the stiff piece of brocade that she appears to be in her first lines. She comes to realize that America will not find faith through scholastic syllogistic reasoning, but through "objects of sight instead of words" (407), the "sensate experimentalism" practiced by Sor Juana herself in her search for truth. Yet what Religion gives to America *is* words in a play, the symbols that mediate between language and experience. In the Counter-Reformation, that is the best that Religion can do for those who cry out for direct experience of their gods. Religion feels obligated to rein in America's "freer expression of her intuition," and America's admirable verbal courage sometimes proves insufficient in the face of military and ecclesiastical power. At times, these characters, apparent polar opposites, seem to be acting out a *psychomachia* occurring in the mind of their author. The audience can hardly be entirely surprised, then, when the identities of Religion and America seem to merge at the end of the *loa*, (ll. 480–88), where both women characters take the role of author in the conventional apology for the *auto*.

Twentieth-century multicultural hindsight might find Sor Juana guilty of coercing her characters to accept Religion's reading of reality by the end of the *loa*. However, the author's characterization and apportioning of heroic rhetoric and moving poetry to the Aztecs before their inevitable conversions indicate that she understood well the faults of Zeal and the self-deceptions of her own Religion. These she endured in her own life, not always with patience, but with faith in the salvation story that follows in the *auto*.

While the *loa* attests to Sor Juana's intention that her play be presented in Madrid and while there are no records to show that she actually taught young girls at San Jerónimo or coached them in dramatics, it is tempting to accept Octavio Paz' citation of Thomas Gage's *The English American: A New Survey of the West Indies, 1648* (118) with its reference to children's theater in colonial convents as evidence that such productions may have occurred at San Jerónimo. If they did, it is not difficult to imagine the *loa* staged as a recreation in the convent courtyard with a young nun brandishing the sword of Zeal and small female Spanish soldiers chasing tiny Aztecs around the stage to the sound of trumpet calls. There is a long tradition of such convent performances, which reaches back through monastic history and continues even in the present. Performances such as the one I imagine for Sor Juana's *loa* match my own experience as a Catholic school girl for sixteen years and for another sixteen years as a professor in a Catholic women's college associated with a Benedictine motherhouse. I have both witnessed and participated in the impulse born in the context of women's monastic communities to celebrate many events with dramatic readings, skits, pageants, and plays, frequently humorous, sometimes part of traditional exercises and occasionally staged spontaneously. Older Sisters provide an oral history of such events, but convent archives usually preserve materials about the deeds of the Sisters in building institutions, seldom about their recreations. The paucity of manuscripts and historical records of Hrosvitha or the daughter of Lope de Vega point not to the absence of such dramatic productions in convents, but to centuries of undervaluing them by both women and men monastics.

If the *loa* were acted by girls and Sisters, the ironies of conversion by force and male role-playing would be comically accentuated, much as the naughtier deeds of the gods create irony in the induction to *Dido, Queen of Carthage*, written for the boy actors of the Children of St. Paul's by Christopher Marlowe a century earlier. Had the *loa* been played at the Spanish court or in the Corpus Christi pageant, the speeches of the Aztecs on freedom of religion and the conflict between Spanish love of gold and Aztec love and respect for their earth would have constituted one of the earliest examples of anti-colonialist drama. Perhaps that is why there is no record of production in Spain. In Mexico, the austere Archbishop Francisco Aguiar y Seijas had officially proclaimed his aversion to theater. That and his well-known misogyny made presentation of Sor Juana's play in 1689 or 1690 unlikely. A few years later, in 1692, during the famine and Indian uprisings that preoccupied the court, which had before offered the cloistered author protection and encouragement, such a production, especially of the *loa*, was politically impossible.

### 3. *The* Auto Sacramental *with its* Loa *as Baroque Art*

It is true that *The Divine Narcissus* could be read or performed without its *loa*, much as Shakespeare's *The Taming of the Shrew* is usually staged without its induction. In either case, the dramatic experience is much impoverished by the loss. Quintessentially baroque, the play can be usefully compared to El Greco's *The Burial of Count Orgaz*. Like the painting, the Spanish play is multileveled and expands into a space beyond its original frame. In both baroque works, the action that takes place in the mythic or heavenly sphere is grounded in the everyday and personal experience located below and contained within the earthly frame.

In El Greco's painting, at the lower level, local particularities are mixed with legend. The body of the count is lowered into the grave by Saints Stephen and Augustine, who were said to have appeared to Count Orgaz in his lifetime. The figures of the mourners are portraits of contemporary nobles and clergy, among them, a self-portrait of the artist. El Greco humorously identifies the acolyte wearing a handkerchief lettered "Domenicos Théotocópoulous made me, 1578 [the date of his son's birth]" (Fleming 271).

With its Mexican history, the *loa* is parallel to this level, and like El Greco's portrait of his son, it contains its own autobiographical "signature": Religion's protest to Zeal that she writes only in obedience to her superiors is a statement Sor Juana repeats in *The Answer*.

Both works accentuate the role of Mary as the way to Jesus. At mid-level in the painting, the soul of the count approaches the Virgin Mother on its way to the radiant Christ, who occupies the upper region of the painting where space seems to melt into infinity. In the *Narcissus* plot, Human Nature's image must be reflected in the pure waters of the fountain, which is Mary. Only then will Narcissus/Christ, gazing into the waters, see the face of Human Nature reflecting His own image, causing Him to die for love. At the end of the *auto*, Narcissus rises from the dead and ascends into the same radiant heaven as El Greco's Christ. Narcissus/Christ also escapes time and space by His mystical presence in the Eucharist.

Besides mirroring the multileveled universe of the baroque painting, the play also provides a multicultural perspective replete with the extreme contrasts that give energy to much baroque art. Anticipating the Mary-fountain of the *auto* is a more human image submerged in the *loa*. Unlike El Greco's Spanish Virgin, Sor Juana's cultural image of Mary is American, The Virgin of Guadalupe, who appeared on the *tilma* (cloak) of Juan Diego in 1521:

> She has the dark complexion, hair and eyes of the Aztec. She is not like the "white" Virgin of the Spaniards. She is standing in front of and blocking the sun, one of the most powerful of the Aztec gods. By this she conveyed to the Indians that she was more powerful than even their sun god. She stands upon a blackened, burned-out crescent moon showing that she is more powerful than the great moon god. . . . Her clothing is brightly colored blue-green and rose, colors which had been reserved to Aztec royalty. . . . Around her waist she wore a black sash. This sash was the symbol of a woman who had born a child. . . . To the conquered Aztecs the Lady's meaning was clear. She was the Mother of all, but especially the mother of the Son whom she had come to announce. (Freeman 7)

This is the Virgin of Mexico, the setting of the *loa*, and there the Virgin looks more like Sor Juana's America than El Greco's pale Mary. During Sor Juana's time, devotion to The Virgin of Guadalupe was popular and intense, and the appearance of America in her Aztec costume and demeanor would immediately evoke connections to the American Virgin Mary.

Even as they suggest the culturally contrasting Marian images, the *loa* and the *auto* link European traditional culture, with its emphases on ancient Mediterranean classical literature and pure blood lines, to the emerging Mexican nation, which will draw its strength and beauty from a *mestizo* population of many traditions and races. Sor Juana is a *criolla*, a Mexican woman whose genetic and literary heritage originates in the New World with its own pagan myths and rituals only recently forcibly supplemented by the Spanish Christianity of the Old World. Intellectually, she is devoted to her European past. Within herself she achieves the combination of opposites reflected in the contrasting settings, cultures, and races of the *loa* and *auto*, a combination so characteristic of baroque art.

When she changes the setting to Spain for the *auto*, Sor Juana turns to more European materials for her mythic level, again combining pagan and Christian stories to express their common truth. From Ovid's *Metamorphoses* she takes the tragic tale of the beautiful youth Narcissus, loved in vain by the nymph Echo. Because she talks too much and aids Jupiter in his adulterous plots, Echo is punished by Juno, and is then unable to express her love, but can only repeat the final words of others. Inarticulate and ignored by Narcissus, Echo pines until nothing remains of her but her voice. Narcissus comes to a similar end when he falls in love with his own reflection in a fountain. He too languishes, he dies, and his body changes into a white flower, the narcissus.

## 4. *The Divine Narcissus* as American Feminist Art

Sor Juana's play gives birth to a feminine and American version of the story of redemption, what Stephanie Merrim calls a "womanscript" because of its many strong female characters and themes. Inspired by Calderón's *Pastor Fido* and his *Eco and Narciso* and surpassing them (Trueblood 20), Sor Juana's treatment of the Ovidian myth is original in its conflation of Narcissus with Christ, the identification of Echo with Satan, and the exploration of the difference between the creative use of traditional sources and the echoing of previous works that is merely derivative. Sor Juana uses the pagan Ovid, the Judeo-Christian Scriptures, and other texts as the seeds to form her Narcissus/Christ. She redeems her hero from the fabled lonely egotism of Ovid's story by causing Him to see the reflection of Human Nature, who is His image, and to die for her. The only other male figure, Self-love, provides a direct contrast with the selfless love of Sor Juana's passionate shepherd-God who seems to be more closely related to *"El Pastorcico"* of St. John of the Cross than to Ovid's character. His language comes mostly from the Epistles and Gospels, the daily readings of the Mass, and from Isaiah, the Canticle of Canticles, and the Psalms that have always constituted most of the prayers in the Liturgy of the Hours, recited throughout each day by nuns. Thus, Sor Juana knew many of Narcissus' speeches by heart long before she set them into the play, but she molds her sources, which also constitute her prayer-life, into new and surprising combinations. Biblical literature is reframed as a pastoral love story in which women are important, active, and effective participants.

Octavio Paz believes that the idea to substitute the reflection of Human Nature for Narcissus' own may have come from the *Pimander*, the first book of the *Corpus Hermeticum* (352). But Sor Juana's character differs significantly from *Pimander*'s Nature. Unlike the heroines of most pastorals, but much like Sor Juana's mother, Isabel Ramírez, Human Nature is the unmarried mother of daughters. At first, tempted into sin by the jealous Echo, Human Nature cannot reflect Narcissus' face in the muddy waters of her sinfulness:

> And for those reasons do I call
> my evil muddy waters too,
> whose darkly-colored murkiness
> so separates my Love from me.
> (233–36)

The image is remarkably similar to one recorded in the *Life* of St. Teresa, whom Sor Juana calls in *The Answer* "my own mother Teresa":

> On one occasion, when I was reciting the Hours with the community, my soul suddenly became recollected and seemed to me to become bright all over like a mirror; no part of it— back, sides, top or bottom—but was completely bright, and in the center of it was a picture of Christ Our Lord. . . . It was explained to me that, when a soul is in mortal sin, this mirror is covered with a thick mist and remains darkened so that the Lord cannot be pictured or seen in it. (390)

St. Teresa's vision, in reverse order, is what Human Nature experiences in the beginning of the play. By the end, redeemed Human Nature reflects the face of Christ exactly as in St. Teresa's vision. Once again, Sor Juana's inspiration comes from her life as a nun. Her three months with the Carmelites gave her a lasting love for Saint Teresa and Saint John of the Cross (Juan de la Cruz), whose name she bears in its feminine form.

Led by Grace, her affectionate childhood friend, Human Nature's soul can become bright enough to reflect her Narcissus/Christ only by being cleansed of her darkness in the crystal waters of baptism flowing from the fountain who is Mary. Both the sacrilege of sin and the sacrament of baptism, both the power to tempt and the means of grace are in the hands of female figures. From a feminist point of view, Sor Juana's myth is a decided improvement on the Book of Genesis, where Eve commits the first sin and then tempts Adam to sin with her. Like the Greek Pandora, Eve/woman thus is held responsible by the patriarchal text for the evils that befall humankind.

In *The Divine Narcissus*, Satan himself bears the name and wears the costume of a woman, Echo. In the love triangle of Human Nature, Echo, and Narcissus, Sor Juana re-visions Echo as a satanic temptress, not a victim. Merrim may be right that the self-conscious Echo who tells stories and is finally silenced represents in some ways patriarchally subdued women writers like Sor Juana (114–15). Sor Juana does seem to gaze into her own mirror at times when she is creating characters, and her features can be found sketched into more than one. Human Nature, for instance, appears at the beginning of the play as a woman with the problem of reconciling opposites, in this case, her daughters, Gentile and Synagogue. Human Nature solves the problem exactly as her creator Sor Juana does: she rewrites the Echo and Narcissus myth.

If Human Nature is Sor Juana's fictional stand-in, is Echo her alter-ego? The stories Echo tells are not her own, but Satan's, whose art is destructive. He is the fallen angel, "dissolute and damned,"

> whose daring dragged to the Abyss
> a third part of the weeping stars;
> (347–50)

And his Echo is merely a "costume," which barely covers his own identity. He, in turn, has stolen the idea for a refashioned Echo from Human Nature, as he explains to the audience. Like a serpent, his speech of over two hundred lines uncoils, revealing not only Human Nature's earlier creative refashioning of Ovid's plot, but his own response—a great act of plagiarism:

> . . . and following a metaphor
> identical to hers [Human Nature's], I want
> to fashion yet another nymph,
> who follows her Narcissus, for
> whatever role could I play now
> but an unhappy Echo who
> laments Narcissus constantly?
> (351–57)

The situation elucidates the difference between our understanding of originality and that of authors of the sixteenth and seventeenth centuries. Much like Shakespeare, Calderón, and Sor Juana, Human Nature has combined well-known classical and biblical sources as well as some contemporary materials to craft her own play, and then Human Nature has given herself the female leading part. Sor Juana adds more than one original twist. Human Nature is not the only author, but one of a committee of fictional female authors for the *auto*, including America and Religion. She adds as well a plagiarist who doesn't copy mere words. Satan, by stealing the metaphor of the nymph, tries to plagiarize the entire story by acting the stolen part in it. Echo/Satan fails, not for lack of cleverness, but for lack of creativity. S/he can only repeat exactly what others write or say, and less and less of that as the play moves through Mexico,

Ovid, salvation history narrated in both testaments of Scripture, and echoes of Spanish literary texts, to its conclusion, the hymn of Saint Thomas Aquinas honoring the Eucharist.

In Sor Juana's *loa* and *auto*, originality does not lie in either abolishing patriarchal texts or merely echoing them, which is satanic, but in re-visioning them in terms of female experience. Thus the pronoun reference for Human Nature becomes the generic *she*, and the canonical texts of the synagogue and pagan antiquity are recast as female like Grace itself, the Christian's sharing in the life of the Divine Narcissus, Who wins redemption for Human Nature. Nevertheless, redemption becomes accessible only through the communal efforts of women, Human Nature, Grace, and Mary, whose cooperation makes redemptive love possible. (In "Speaking the Mother Tongue," Electa Arenal calls her "Mary, Creator of the Word" and asserts that Sor Juana parallels her "with woman writer writing" 99). Their triangular friendship defeats the unholy trinity of Echo-Satan and her/his cohorts, Pride and Self-Love. In the end, Narcissus goes to the throne of His Father and leaves behind, not a bridegroom, but a sacrament. His indwelling Eucharistic presence remains with the women who, like three graces or a small community of Sisters, kneel together around the flower of the "lofty mystery."

Here author-ity is not the tryst of a lone caucasian male with his muse. Rather, with the active help of Grace and Marian receptivity, the power of the Word is shared by both Spanish Religion and Aztec America, by Human Nature and her daughters Synagogue and Gentile—a multicultural sisterhood of writers. Perhaps Sor Juana, self-taught and lonely scholar, besieged woman writer, and Sister hoped her play would prove prophetic.

### The Translation

Until now, an English translation of *The Divine Narcissus* in its entirety has not been published. The *loa* has been translated into English prose by Willis K. Jones and may be found in *Spanish-American Literature in Translation* (New York: Frederick Ungar, 1966), Vol. 1, 301–8; and into English poetry by Margaret Sayers Peden in her *Sor Juana Inés de la Cruz: Poems* (New York: Bilingual Press, 1985), 88–127. An English translation by Alan S. Trueblood of selections from *The Divine Narcissus* appears in his *A Sor Juana Anthology* (Cambridge, Mass.: Harvard University

Press, 1988), 148–65. These translators are also editors of their volumes.

This translation is intended chiefly for students engaged in literary studies or theater. Its primary goal is not to transmute Spanish baroque verse into English baroque verse, a performance which would have few readers. Instead, it attempts to produce a dramatic language that respects the play's cultural roots but also takes into account the twentieth-century English-speaking audience. Except for calculated effect, it avoids poetic inversions. It has altered punctuation to delineate relatively self-contained rhetorical units and to make clear the relationships between complex clauses within the long, often convoluted baroque sentences. It also attempts to translate into sentences that replicate the rhythms of human speech in English and that can be executed by actors of average lung capacity, hopefully without damage to the complexity of Sor Juana's thought or poetic intent.

Rhyme and rhythm convey Sor Juana's artistry, subtlety, passion, and humor. English is a language that has lost much of its inflection and therefore much of its capacity to rhyme as easily as Spanish. The English poetic line is more precise and less flexible than Sor Juana's Spanish. The translation attempts to imitate as far as possible the rhythm and rhyme patterns of the original verses, but abandons that effort when it seems to interfere with the meaning or lyricism of the original. Baroque poetry has a tendency to widen and expand, much like the steps of the Laurentian library, repeating and broadening the image as it descends to its end punctuation. Although the length of the translation is the same as the original, sometimes it has expanded on images by variation rather than by baroque forms of repetition. In the *auto*, Sor Juana displays her virtuosity in a showcase of Spanish verse forms, the *endecha, lira, décima, soneto,* and *romance.* In each example of these, particular attention is paid to form and rhythm. In the *loa*, poetry is not so varied, and so the nine- to thirteen-syllable Spanish lines translate fairly uniformly into iambic tetrameter.

Vocabulary choices and ways of using rhyme to translate Sor Juana's characters vary in order to interpret them in English. For example, a somewhat starched vocabulary, some alliteration, occasional inverted word order, and sometimes more rhyme than the original text indicates, often double rhymes and sometimes internal rhymes underline Zeal's rather old-fashioned, chivalric, but slightly ridiculous character. Similar techniques are applied to convey the absurdity of Self-love and the pompousness of Pride. Their vocabularies may be pretentious, but the rhymes are often calculated to prick the rhetoric and deflate it. Their syntax can be more convoluted than their simple-mindedness seems to warrant, and that sinuous syntax is intensified by Sor Juana's use of long, windy asides to the audience, further explaining and further complicating their ideas. In such cases, the translator ought not to interfere with excessive clarity. By contrast, Narcissus speaks an elevated but heroic style, and when His speeches quote well-known scriptural passages, we use the vocabulary of familiar translations whenever possible.

The themes of mirroring and echoing in the play suggest the art of translation itself. How should one translate literary echoes in the text of the author? Sor Juana's poetic borrowings include quotations, direct and indirect, from her favorite literary contemporaries. The occasional chords from Calderón or Lope are transposed into phrases or techniques of Marlowe, Shakespeare, Milton, and other English writers.

No attempt has been made, however, to mirror the accidentals of Méndez Plancarte's Spanish text. Orthography is not reproduced. Capitalization and punctuation are silently altered according to modern English usage and in accordance with meaning. Personal pronouns referring to the Judeo-Christian God are capitalized; when they refer to a pagan god or an ordinary mortal, they are in lower case.

Méndez Plancarte's scene divisions have been retained, but his divisions into acts have been omitted. Neither appears in the first editions of the play. Mistakes in his line numbering have been corrected so that line numbers will match in Spanish and English texts.

Stage directions in the original are placed in parentheses. Where stage directions seemed insufficiently clear, they have been expanded and additions are enclosed in square brackets. In addition, where stage directions in Spanish do not appear to accurately reflect the action on the stage they have been silently corrected in the English translation.

## Works Cited

Abreu Gómez, Ermilo. *Sor Juana Inés de la Cruz, Biografía y biblioteca.* Mexico City: Secretaría de Relaciones Exteriores, 1934.

Ackerman, Diane. *Reverse Thunder: A Dramatic Poem.* New York: Lumen Books, 1988.

Arenal, Electa. "Aria of a Cloistered Feminist." Review of *Sor Juana or, the Traps of Faith* by Octavio Paz, Trans. by Margaret Sayers

Peden; *A Sor Juana Anthology*, Trans. by Alan S. Trueblood; *Sor Juana's Dream*, Trans., Introduction and Commentary by Luis Harss. *Commonweal* 27 January 1989: 50–52.

———. "Sor Juana Inés de la Cruz: Speaking the Mother Tongue." *The University of Dayton Review* 16, no.2 (Spring 1983): 93–105.

Augustine, Saint, Bishop of Hippo. *The Rule of Saint Augustine*. Trans. Raymond Canning OSA. London: Darton, Longman & Todd, 1984.

Bradley, Ritamary. "In the Jaws of the Bear: Journeys of Transformation by Women Mystics." *Vox Benedictina* 8, no.1 (Summer 1991): 116–75.

Cvitanovic, Dinko. "Una formulación alegórica en el barroco hispanoamericano." *Teatro de siglo de oro: homenaje a Alberto Navarro González*. Estudios de literatura 7. Kassel: Edition Reichenberger, 1990. 95–108.

Daniel, Lee A. *The Loa of Sor Juana Inés de la Cruz*. Fredericton, Canada: York Press Ltd, 1994.

Fleming, William. *Arts and Ideas*. 6th ed. New York: Holt, Rinehart, & Winston, 1980.

Freeman, Eileen. "Roses in December: The Iconography of Advent." *Modern Liturgy* 5 (November 1978): 6–7.

Graves, Robert. "Juana Inés de la Cruz," *Encounter: Literature, Arts, Politics* 1, no.3 (December, 1953): 5–13.

Juana Inés de la Cruz. *The Answer/La Respuesta*. Trans. and ed. Electa Arenal and Amanda Powell. New York: The Feminist Press at the City University of New York, 1994.

Lavrin, Asunción. "Sor Juana, Nuns and Nunneries in Baroque Mexico." Conference: Sor Juana and the Age of the Baroque, at UCLA, May 19, 1995.

———. "Unlike Sor Juana?: The Model Nun in the Religious Literature of Colonial Mexico." *University of Dayton Review* 16, no.2 (Spring 1983): 75–92.

———. "Values and Meaning of Monastic Life for Nuns in Colonial Mexico." *The Catholic Historical Review* 58 (October 1972): 367–87.

McKendrick, Melveena. *Theater in Spain, 1490–1700*. Cambridge, England: Cambridge University Press, 1989.

Merrim, Stephanie. "*Mores Geometricae*: the Womanscript in the Theater of Sor Juana Inés de la Cruz." *Feminist Perspectives on Sor Juana Inés de la Cruz*. Ed. Stephanie Merrim. Detroit: Wayne State University Press, 1991. 94–123.

*Native Mesoamerican Spirituality*. Ed. Miguel Léon-Portilla. The Classics of Western Spirituality 37. New York: Paulist Press, 1980.

Paz, Octavio. *Sor Juana or, The Traps of Faith*. Trans. Margaret Sayers Peden. Cambridge: Mass.: Harvard University Press, 1988.

Pfandl, Ludwig. *Juana Inés de la Cruz, la décima musa de México: su vida, su poesía, su psique*. Trans. Juan Antonio Ortega Medina. Mexico City: Universidad Nacional Autónoma de México, 1963.

Tavard, George H. *Juana Inés de la Cruz and the Theology of Beauty*. Indiana: Notre Dame University Press, 1991.

Teresa of Avila, Saint. *The Life of Teresa of Avila*. Trans. and ed. E. Allison Peers. New York: Image Books, 1960.

# Acknowledgments

Women's projects are seldom "master-pieces," but usually community-pieces. This book had the good fortune to be conceived and birthed at the College of St. Benedict, in the shadow of the monastery of the Sisters of St. Benedict. Beneath the chapel dome, I have experienced instruction as an oblate, inspiring liturgy as a participant, many a delicious meal as a guest–friend, and the sense of stability which is inherent in the Benedictine Rule. The Community gave me my project partner and friend, Sister Renée Domeier. I am indebted to the College as well for its supporting this work with a sabbatical leave and grant money to travel to libraries and conferences, to the English department for its material assistance, and especially to the department secretary, Beverly Radaich, who worked many long hours on the manuscript. Professor Elena Sánchez-Mora of Modern and Classical Languages, Sister Mara Faulkner and Sister Sheila Rausch, professors of English, and the students of English 335 generously read drafts and offered careful, helpful critiques. I want also to thank Professor Fred Fornoff, past president of the American Literary Translators' Association, whose generous expenditure of time and effort I could not have dispensed with; Father Vernon Meyer of Kino Institute, Phoenix, Arizona, whose biblical scholarship proved a helpful aid as the project concluded; and the Fondo Cultura Económica for permission to use the Spanish text of *El Divino Narciso* (*Obras Completas*, vol. 3, ed. Alfonso Méndez Plancarte, pp. 3-97). Finally, I'd like to thank Barbara Guth and Elizabeth Varnedoe of the University of New Mexico Press for their work and encouragement, from manuscript to printed pages.

PATRICIA A. PETERS

I acknowledge with gratitude the contributions of the Benedictine community that has formed me and supported me these many years.

I am indebted to a number of gifted teachers and colleagues who have offered counsel, expertise, moral support, and above all love. I wish to mention especially:

> my co-author, Pat Peters, who made this publication possible for both of us. I particularly commend her in her ability to make an exquisite piece of baroque poetry an equally elegant and readable literary piece for twentieth century readers;

> other valued colleagues including Monroe Z. Hafter, Francisco Elvira-Hernández, Bob and Mary Joyce, Marina Martín, Lisa Ohm, Jim O'Neill, Jana Preble, Tey Diana Rebolledo, Patricia O. Steiner, Sisters Kathleen Kalinowski, Linnea Welter, and Stefanie Weisgram.

Finally, and always, I am deeply grateful to my father, Charles Domeier, and my deceased mother, Rose, for their inspirational support.

RENÉE DOMEIER, O.S.B.

# The Divine Narcissus
## *El Divino Narciso*

# Loa para el auto sacramental de El Divino Narciso
## por alegorías

PERSONAS QUE HABLAN EN ELLA

El Occidente        La Religión
La América         Músicos
El Celo            Soldados

---

## ESCENA I

(Sale el Occidente, Indio galán, con corona, y la América, a su lado, de India bizarra: con mantas y cupiles, al modo que se canta el Tocotín. Siéntanse en dos sillas; y por una parte y otra bailan Indios e Indias, con plumas y sonajas en las manos, como se hace de ordinario esta Danza; y mientras bailan, canta la Música.)

*Música*

Nobles Mejicanos,
cuya estirpe antigua,
de las claras luces
del Sol se origina:
pues hoy es del año
el dichoso día
en que se consagra
la mayor Reliquia,
¡venid adornados
de vuestras divisas,            10
y a la devoción
se una la alegría;
y en pompa festiva,
celebrad al gran Dios de las Semillas!

*Música*

Y pues la abundancia
de nuestras provincias

# The Loa for the Auto Sacramental of The Divine Narcissus
## an allegory

SPEAKING CHARACTERS

| | |
|---|---|
| Occident | Religion |
| America | Musician |
| Zeal | Soldiers |

---

## SCENE 1

(Enter Occident, a gallant-looking Aztec, wearing a crown. By his side is America, an Aztec woman of poised self-possession. They are dressed in the *mantas* and *huipiles* worn for singing a *tocotín*. They seat themselves on two chairs. On each side, Aztec men and women dance with feathers and rattles in their hands, as is customary for those doing this dance. While they dance, Music sings.)

*Music*

> O, Noble Mexicans,
> whose ancient ancestry
> comes forth from the clear light
> and brilliance of the Sun,
> since this, of all the year,
> is your most happy feast
> in which you venerate
> your greatest deity,
> come and adorn yourselves
> with vestments of your rank;    10
> let your holy fervor be
> made one with jubilation;
> and celebrate in festive pomp
> the great God of the Seeds!

*Music*

> Since the abundance of
> our native fields and farms

se Le debe al que es
Quien las fertiliza,
ofreced devotos,
pues Le son debidas,                                        20
de los nuevos frutos
todas las primicias.
¡Dad de vuestras venas
la sangre más fina,
para que, mezclada,
a su culto sirva;
y en pompa festiva,
celebrad al gran Dios de las Semillas!

(Siéntanse el Occidente y la América, y cesa la Música.)

### Occidente

Pues entre todos los Dioses
que mi culto solemniza,                                     30
aunque son tantos, que sólo
en aquesta esclarecida
Ciudad Regia, de dos mil
pasan, a quien sacrifica
en sacrificios crüentos
de humana sangre vertida,
ya las entrañas que pulsan,
ya el corazón que palpita;
aunque son (vuelvo a decir)
tantos, entre todos mira                                    40
mi atención, como a mayor,
al gran Dios de las Semillas.

### América

Y con razón, pues es solo
el que nuestra Monarquía
sustenta, pues la abundancia
de los frutos se Le aplica;
y como éste es el mayor
beneficio, en quien se cifran
todos los otros, pues lo es
el de conservar la vida,                                    50
como el mayor Lo estimamos:
pues ¿qué importara que rica

is owed to him alone
who gives fertility,
then offer him your thanks,
for it is right and just                          20
to give from what has grown,
the first of the new fruits.
From your own veins, draw out
and give, without reserve,
the best blood, mixed with seed,
so that his cult be served,
and celebrate in festive pomp,
the great God of the Seeds!

(Occident and America sit, and Music ceases.)

### Occident

Of all the deities to whom
our rites demand I bend my knee—                  30
among two thousand gods or more
who dwell within this royal city
and who require the sacrifice
of human victims still entreating
for life until their blood is drawn
and gushes forth from hearts still beating
and bowels still pulsing—I declare,
among all these, (it bears repeating),
whose ceremonies we observe,
the greatest is, surpassing all                   40
this pantheon's immensity
the great God of the Seeds.

### America

And you are right, since he alone
daily sustains our monarchy
because our lives depend on his
providing crops abundantly;
and since he gives us graciously
the gift from which all gifts proceed,
our fields rich with golden maize,
the source of life through daily bread,           50
we render him our highest praise.
Then how will it improve our lives

el América abundara
en el oro de sus minas,
si esterilizando el campo
sus fumosidades mismas,
no dejaran a los frutos
que en sementeras opimas
brotasen? Demás de que
su protección no limita                               60
sólo a corporal sustento
de la material comida,
sino que después, haciendo
manjar de sus carnes mismas
(estando purificadas
antes, de sus inmundicias
corporales), de las manchas
el Alma nos purifica.
Y así, atentos a su culto,
todos conmigo repitan:                                70

*Ellos, y Música*

¡En pompa festiva,
celebrad al gran Dios de las Semillas!

---

## Escena II

(Éntranse bailando; y salen la Religión Cristiana, de Dama Española, y el Celo, de Capitán General, armado; y detrás, Soldados Españoles.)

*Religión*

¿Cómo, siendo el Celo tú,
sufren tus cristianas iras
ver que, vanamente ciega,
celebre la Idolatría
con supersticiosos cultos
un Ídolo, en ignominia
de la Religión Cristiana?

if rich America abounds
in gold from mines whose smoke deprives
the fields of their fertility
and with their clouds of filthy soot
will not allow the crops to grow
which blossom now so fruitfully
from seeded earth? Moreover, his
protection of our people far
exceeds our daily food and drink,                    60
the body's sustenance. Indeed,
he feeds us with his very flesh
(first purified of every stain).
We eat his body, drink his blood,
and by this sacred meal are freed
and cleansed from all that is profane,
and thus, he purifies our soul.
And now, attentive to his rites,
together let us all proclaim:                         70

They *[Occident, America, Dancers]* and Music

we celebrate in festive pomp,
the great God of the Seeds!

---

## Scene 2

(They exit dancing. Enter Christian Religion as a Spanish lady,
Zeal as a Captain General in armor, and Spanish soldiers.)

*Religion*

How, being Zeal, can you suppress
the flames of righteous Christian wrath
when here before your very eyes
idolatry, so blind with pride,
adores, with superstitious rites
an idol, leaving your own bride,
the holy faith of Christ disgraced?

### Celo

Religión: no tan aprisa          80
de mi omisión te querelles,
te quejes de mis caricias;
pues ya levantado el brazo,
ya blandida la cuchilla
traigo, para tus venganzas.
Tú a ese lado te retira
mientras vengo tus agravios.

(Salen, bailando, el Occidente y América, y Acompañamiento y Música, por otro lado.)

### Música

¡Y en pompa festiva,
celebrad al gran Dios de las Semillas!

### Celo

Pues ya ellos salen, yo llego.       90

### Religión

Yo iré también, que me inclina
la piedad a llegar (antes
que tu furor los embista)
a convidarlos, de paz,
a que mi culto reciban.

### Celo

Pues lleguemos, que en sus torpes
ritos está entretenida.

### Música

¡Y en pompa festiva,
celebrad al gran Dios de las Semillas!

(Llegan el Celo y la Religión.)

### Religión

Occidente poderoso,       100
América bella y rica,
que vivís tan miserables
entre las riquezas mismas:

### Zeal

Religion, trouble not your mind                           80
or grieve my failure to attack,
complaining that my love is slack,
for now the sword I wear is bared,
its hilt in hand, clasped ready and
my arm raised high to take revenge.
Please stand aside and deign to wait
till I requite your grievances.

(Enter Occident and America dancing, and accompanied by Music, who enters from the other side.)

### Music

And celebrate in festive pomp,
the great God of the Seeds!

### Zeal

Here they come!  I will confront them.                    90

### Religion

And I, in peace, will also go
(before your fury lays them low)
for justice must with mercy kiss;
I shall invite them to arise
from superstitious depths to faith.

### Zeal

Let us approach while they are still
absorbed in their lewd rituals.

### Music

And celebrate in festive pomp,
the great God of the Seeds!

(Zeal and Religion cross the stage.)

### Religion

Great Occident, most powerful;                            100
America, so beautiful
and rich; you live in poverty
amid the treasures of your land.

dejad el culto profano
a que el Demonio os incita.
¡Abrid los ojos! Seguid
la verdadera Doctrina
que mi amor os persüade.

### Occidente

¿Qué gentes no conocidas
son éstas que miro, ¡Cielos!,                    110
que así de mis alegrías
quieren impedir el curso?

### América

¿Qué Naciones nunca vistas
quieren oponerse al fuero
de mi potestad antigua?

### Occidente

¡Oh tú, extranjera Belleza;
¡oh tú, Mujer peregrina!
Díme quién eres, que vienes
a perturbar mis delicias.

### Religión

Soy la Religión Cristiana                        120
que intento que tus Provincias
se reduzcan a mi culto.

### Occidente

¡Buen empeño solicitas!

### América

¡Buena locura pretendes!

### Occidente

¡Buen imposible maquinas!

### América

Sin duda es loca; ¡dejadla,
y nuestros cultos prosigan!

Abandon this irreverent cult
with which the demon has waylaid you.
Open your eyes!  Follow the path
that leads straightforwardly to truth,
to which my love yearns to persuade you.

### Occident

Who are these unknown people, so
intrusive in my sight, who dare                    110
to stop us in our ecstasy?
Heaven forbid such infamy!

### America

Who are these nations, never seen,
that wish, by force, to pit themselves
against my ancient power supreme?

### Occident

Oh, you alien beauty fair;
oh, pilgrim woman from afar,
who comes to interrupt my prayer,
please speak and tell me who you are.

### Religion

Christian Religion is my name,                    120
and I intend that all this realm
will make obeisance unto me.

### Occident

An impossible concession!

### America

Yours is but a mad obsession!

### Occident

You will meet with swift repression.

### America

Pay no attention; she is mad!
Let us go on with our procession.

### Música y Ellos

¡Y en pompa festiva,
celebrad al gran Dios de las Semillas!

### Celo

¿Cómo, bárbaro Occidente;                    130
cómo, ciega Idolatría,
a la Religión desprecias,
mi dulce Esposa querida?
Pues mira que a tus maldades
ya has llenado la medida,
y que no permite Dios
que en tus delitos prosigas,
y me envía a castigarte.

### Occidente

¿Quién eres, que atemorizas
con sólo ver tu semblante?                    140

### Celo

El Celo soy. ¿Qué te admira?
Que, cuando a la Religión
desprecian tus demasías,
entrará el Celo a vengarla
castigando tu osadía.
Ministro de Dios soy, que
viendo que tus tiranías
han llegado ya a lo sumo,
cansado de ver que vivas
tantos años entre errores,                    150
a castigarte me envía.
Y así, estas armadas Huestes,
que rayos de acero vibran,
ministros son de Su enojo
e instrumentos de Sus iras.

### Occidente

¿Qué Dios, qué error, qué torpeza,
o qué castigos me intimas?
Que no entiendo tus razones
ni aun por remotas noticias,
ni quién eres tú, que osado                    160

*Music and all* [Aztecs on stage]

And celebrate in festive pomp,
the great God of the Seeds!

### Zeal

How is this, barbarous Occident?                    130
Can it be, sightless Idolatry,
that you insult Religion,
the spouse I cherish tenderly?
Abomination fills your cup
and overruns the brim, but see
that God will not permit you to
continue drinking down delight,
and I am sent to deal your doom.

### Occident

And who are you who frightens all
who only look upon your face?                       140

### Zeal

I am Zeal. Does that surprise you?
Take heed! for when your excesses
bring disgrace to fair Religion,
then will Zeal arise to vengeance;
for insolence I will chastise you.
I am the minister of God,
Who growing weary with the sight
of overreaching tyrannies
so sinful that they reach the height
of error, practiced many years,               150
has sent me forth to penalize you.
And thus, these military hosts
with flashing thunderbolts of steel,
the ministers of His great wrath
are sent, His anger to reveal.

### Occident

What god? What sin? What tyranny?
What punishment do you foresee?
Your reasons make no sense to me,
nor can I make the slightest guess
who you might be with your insistence         160

a tanto empeño te animas
como impedir que mi gente
en debidos cultos diga:

*Música*

¡Y en pompa festiva,
celebrad al gran Dios de las Semillas!

*América*

Bárbaro, loco, que ciego,
con razones no entendidas,
quieres turbar el sosiego
que en serena paz tranquila
gozamos: ¡cesa en tu intento,                    170
si no quieres que, en cenizas
reducido, ni aun los vientos
tengan de tu sér noticias!
Y tú, Esposo, y tus vasallos,

(Al Occidente)

negad el oído y vista
a sus razones, no haciendo
caso de sus fantasías;
y proseguid vuestros cultos,
sin dejar que advenedizas
Naciones, osadas quieran                          180
intentar interrumpirlas.

*Música*

¡Y en pompa festiva,
celebrad al gran Dios de las Semillas!

*Celo*

Pues la primera propuesta
de paz desprecias altiva,
la segunda, de la guerra,
será preciso que admitas.
¡Toca al arma! ¡Guerra, guerra!

(Suenan cajas y clarines.)

on tolerating no resistance,
impeding us with rash persistence
from lawful worship as we sing.

### Music

And celebrate with festive pomp,
the great God of the Seeds!

### America

Madman, blind, and barbarous,
with mystifying messages
you try to mar our calm and peace,
destroying the tranquility
that we enjoy.  Your plots must cease,                170
unless, of course, you wish to be
reduced to ashes, whose existence
even the winds will never sense.

(to Occident)

And you, my spouse, and your cohort,
close off your hearing and your sight
to all their words; refuse to heed
their fantasies of zealous might;
proceed to carry out your rite.
Do not concede to insolence
from foreigners intent to dull                        180
our ritual's magnificence.

### Music

And celebrate with festive pomp,
the great God of the Seeds!

### Zeal

Since our initial offering
of peaceful terms, you held so cheap,
the dire alternative of war,
I guarantee you'll count more dear.
Take up your arms! To war! To war!

(Drums and trumpets sound.)

*Occidente*

¿Qué abortos el Cielo envía
contra mí? ¿Qué armas son éstas,                    190
nunca de mis ojos vistas?
¡Ah, de mis Guardas! ¡Soldados:
las flechas que prevenidas
están siempre, disparad!

*América*

¿Qué rayos el Cielo vibra
contra mí? ¿Qué fieros globos
de plomo ardiente graniza?
¿Qué Centauros monstrüosos
contra mis gentes militan?

(Dentro)

¡Arma, arma! ¡Guerra, guerra!                       200

(Tocan)

¡Viva España! ¡Su Rey viva!

(Trabada la batalla, van entrándose por una puerta, y salen por
otra huyendo los Indios, y los Españoles en su alcance; y detrás,
el Occidente retirándose de la Religión, y América del Celo.)

---

## Escena III

*Religión*

¡Ríndete, altivo Occidente!

*Occidente*

Ya es preciso que me rinda
tu valor, no tu razón.

*Celo*

¡Muere, América atrevida!

## Occident

What miscarriages of justice
has heaven sent against me?                                    190
What are these weapons, blazing fire,
before my unbelieving eyes?
Get ready, guards!  Aim well, my troops,
Your arrows at this enemy!

## America

What lightening bolts does heaven send
to lay me low?  What molten balls
of burning lead so fiercely rain?
What centaurs crush with monstrous force
and cause my people such great pain?

(Within)

To arms! To arms!  War!  War!                                  200

([Drums and trumpets] sound.)

Long life to Spain!  Long live her king!

(The battle begins.  Indians enter through one door and flee through
another with the Spanish pursuing at their heels.  From back
stage, Occident backs away from Religion and America retreats
before Zeal's onslaught.)

---

# Scene 3

## Religion

Give up, arrogant Occident!

## Occident

I must bow to your aggression,
but not before your arguments.

## Zeal

Die, impudent America!

### Religión

¡Espera, no le des muerte,
que la necesito viva!

### Celo

Pues ¿cómo tú la defiendes,
cuando eres tú la ofendida?

### Religión

Sí, porque haberla vencido                    210
le tocó a tu valentía,
pero a mi piedad le toca
el conservarle la vida:
porque vencerla por fuerza
te tocó; mas el rendirla
con razón, me toca a mí,
con suavidad persuasiva.

### Celo

Si has visto ya la protervia
con que tu culto abominan
ciegos, ¿no es mejor que todos         220
mueran?

### Religión

      Cese tu justicia,
Celo; no les des la muerte:
que no quiere mi benigna
condición, que mueran, sino
que se conviertan y vivan.

### América

Si el pedir que yo no muera,
y el mostrarte compasiva,
es porque esperas de mí
que me vencerás, altiva,
como antes con corporales,              230
después con intelectivas
armas, estás engañada;
pues aunque lloro cautiva
mi libertad, ¡mi albedrío,
con libertad más crecida
adorará mis Deidades!

### Religion

Desist! Do not give her to Death;
her life is of some worth to us.

### Zeal

How can you now defend this maid
who has so much offended you?

### Religion

America has been subdued                           210
because your valor won the strife,
but now my mercy intervenes
in order to preserve her life.
It was your part to conquer her
by force with military might;
mine is to gently make her yield,
persuading her by reason's light.

### Zeal

But you have seen the stubbornness
with which these blind ones still abhor
your creed; is it not better far                    220
that they all die?

### Religion

       Good Zeal, restrain
your justice, and do not kill them.
My gentle disposition deigns
to forbear vengeance and forgive.
I want them to convert and live.

### America

If your petition for my life
and show of Christian charity
are motivated by the hope
that you, at last, will conquer me,
defeating my integrity                              230
with verbal steel where bullets failed,
then you are sadly self-deceived.
A weeping captive, I may mourn
for liberty, yet my will grows
beyond these bonds; my heart is free,
and I will worship my own gods!

*Occidente*

Yo ya dije que me obliga
a rendirme a ti la fuerza;
y en esto, claro se explica
que no hay fuerza ni violencia                     240
que a la voluntad impida
sus libres operaciones;
y así, aunque cautivo gima,
¡no me podrás impedir
que acá, en mi corazón, diga
que venero al gran Dios de las Semillas!

---

## Escena IV

*Religión*

Espera, que aquésta no
es fuerza, sino caricia.
¿Qué Dios es ése que adoras?

*Occidente*

Es un Dios que fertiliza                           250
los campos que dan los frutos;
a quien los cielos se inclinan,
a Quien la lluvia obedece
y, en fin, es El que nos limpia
los pecados, y después
se hace Manjar, que nos brinda.
¡Mira tú si puede haber,
en la Deidad más benigna,
más beneficios que haga
ni más que yo te repita!                           260

*Religión*

(Aparte)

¡Válgame Dios! ¿Qué dibujos,
qué remedos o qué cifras
de nuestras sacras Verdades
quieren ser estas mentiras?

### Occident

Forced to surrender to your power,
I have admitted my defeat,
but still it must be clearly said
that violence cannot devour                           240
my will, nor force constrain its right.
Although in grief, I now lament,
a prisoner, your cruel might
has limits. You cannot prevent
my saying here within my heart
I worship the great God of Seeds!

---

## Scene 4

### Religion

Wait! What you perceive as force
is not coercion, but affection.
What god is this that you adore?

### Occident

The great God of the Seeds                            250
who causes fields to bring forth fruit.
To him the lofty heavens bow;
to him the rains obedience give;
and when, at last, he cleanses us
from stains of sin, then he invites
us to the meal that he prepares.
Consider whether you could find
a god more generous and good
who blesses more abundantly
than he whom I describe to you.                       260

### Religion

(Aside)

O God, help me! What images,
what dark designs, what shadowings
of truths most sacred to our Faith
do these lies seek to imitate?

¡Oh cautelosa Serpiente!
¡Oh Aspid venenoso! ¡Oh Hidra,
que viertes por siete bocas,
de tu ponzoña nociva
toda la mortal cicuta!
¿Hasta dónde tu malicia                          270
quiere remedar de Dios
las sagradas Maravillas?
Pero con tu mismo engaño,
si Dios mi lengua habilita,
te tengo de convencer.

### América

¿En qué, suspensa, imaginas?
¿Ves cómo no hay otro Dios
como Aquéste, que confirma
en beneficios Sus obras?

### Religión

De Pablo con la doctrina                         280
tengo de argüir; pues cuando
a los de Atenas predica,
viendo que entre ellos es ley
que muera el que solicita
introducir nuevos Dioses,
como él tiene la noticia
de que a un *Dios no conocido*
ellos un altar dedican,
les dice: "No es Deidad nueva,
sino la no conocida                              290
que adoráis en este altar,
la que mi voz os publica."
Así yo . . .

¡Occidente, escucha;
oye, ciega Idolatría,
pues en escuchar mis voces
consisten todas tus dichas!
   Esos milagros que cuentas,
esos prodigios que intimas,
esos visos, esos rasgos,

O false, sly, and deceitful snake!
O asp, with sting so venomous!
O hydra, that from seven mouths
pours noxious poisons, every one
a passage to oblivion!
To what extent, with this facade           270
do you intend maliciously
to mock the mysteries of God?
Mock on! for with your own deceit,
if God empowers my mind and tongue,
I'll argue and impose defeat.

### America

Why do you find yourself perplexed?
Do you not see there is no god
other than ours who verifies
with countless blessings his great works?

### Religion

In doctrinal disputes, I hold           280
with the apostle Paul, for when
he preached to the Athenians
and found they had a harsh decree
imposing death on anyone
who tried to introduce new gods,
since he had noticed they were free
to worship at a certain shrine,
an altar to "the Unknown God,"
he said to them, "This Lord of mine
is no new god, but one unknown           290
that you have worshipped in this place,
and it is He, my voice proclaims."
And thus I—

[Occident and America whisper to each other.]

Listen, Occident!
and hear me, blind Idolatry!
for all your happiness depends
on listening attentively.
These miracles that you recount,
these prodigies that you suggest,
these apparitions and these rays

que debajo de cortinas 300
supersticiosas asoman;
esos portentos que vicias,
atribuyendo su efecto
a tus Deidades mentidas,
obras del Dios Verdadero,
y de Su sabiduría
son efectos.  Pues si el prado
florido se fertiliza
si los campos se fecundan,
si el fruto se multiplica, 310
si las sementeras crecen,
si las lluvias se destilan,
todo es obra de Su diestra;
pues ni el brazo que cultiva,
ni la lluvia que fecunda,
ni el calor que vivifica,
diera incremento a las plantas,
a faltar Su productiva
Providencia, que concurre
a darles vegetativa 320
alma.

### América

Cuando eso así sea,
díme: ¿será tan propicia
esa Deidad, que se deje
tocar de mis manos mismas,
como el Ídolo que aquí
mis propias manos fabrican
de semillas y de sangre
inocente, que vertida
es sólo para este efecto?

### Religión

Aunque su Esencia Divina 330
es invisible e inmensa,
como Aquésta está ya unida
a nuestra Naturaleza,
tan Humana se avecina
a nosotros, que permite
que Lo toquen las indignas
manos de los Sacerdotes.

of light in superstition dressed                    300
are glimpsed but darkly through a veil.
These portents you exaggerate,
attributing to your false gods
effects that you insinuate,
but wrongly so, for all these works
proceed from our true God alone,
and of His Wisdom come to birth.
Then if the soil richly yields,
and if the fields bud and bloom,
if fruits increase and multiply,                    310
if seeds mature in earth's dark womb,
if rains pour forth from leaden sky,
all is the work of His right hand;
for neither the arm that tills the soil
nor rains that fertilize the land
nor warmth that calls life from the tomb
of winter's death can make plants grow;
for they lack reproductive power
if Providence does not concur,
by breathing into each of them                      320
a vegetative soul.

### America

       That might be so;
then tell me, is this God so kind—
this deity whom you describe—
that I might touch Him with my hands,
these very hands that carefully
create the idol, here before you,
an image made from seeds of earth
and innocent, pure human blood
shed only for this sacred rite?

### Religion

Although the Essence of Divinity            330
is boundless and invisible,
because already It has been
eternally united with
our nature, He resembles us
so much in our humanity
that He permits unworthy priests
to take Him in their humble hands.

### América

Cuanto a aqueso, convenidas
estamos, porque a mi Dios
no hay nadie a quien se permita                    340
tocarlo, sino a los que
de Sacerdotes Le sirvan;
y no sólo no tocarlo,
mas ni entrar en Su Capilla
se permite a los seglares.

### Celo

¡Oh reverencia, más digna
de hacerse al Dios verdadero!

### Occidente

Y díme, aunque más me digas:
¿será ese Dios, de materias
tan raras, tan exquisitas                          350
como de sangre, que fue
en sacrificio ofrecida,
y semilla, que es sustento?

### Religión

Ya he dicho que es Su infinita
Majestad, inmaterial;
mas Su Humanidad bendita,
puesta incrüenta en el Santo
Sacrificio de la Misa,
en cándidos accidentes,
se vale de las semillas                            360
del trigo, el cual se convierte
en Su Carne y Sangre misma;
y Su Sangre, que en el Cáliz
está, es Sangre que ofrecida
en el Ara de la Cruz,
inocente, pura y limpia,
fue la Redención del Mundo.

### América

Ya que esas tan inauditas
cosas quiera yo creer,
¿será esa Deidad que pintas,                       370

### America

In this, at least, we are agreed,
for to my god no human hands
are so unstained that they deserve                    340
to touch him; nonetheless, he gives
this honor graciously to those
who serve him with their priestly lives.
No others dare to touch the god,
nor in the sanctuary stand.

### Zeal

A reverence most worthily
directed to the one true God!

### Occident

Whatever else you claim, now tell
me this: Is yours a God composed
of human blood, an offering                            350
of sacrifice, and in Himself
does He combine with bloody death
the life-sustaining seeds of earth?

### Religion

As I have said, His boundless
Majesty is insubstantial,
but in the Holy Sacrifice
of Mass, His blessed humanity
is placed unbloody under the
appearances of bread, which comes
from seeds of wheat and is transformed                 360
into His Body and His Blood;
and this most holy Blood of Christ,
contained within a sacred cup,
is verily the offering
most innocent, unstained, and pure
that on the altar of the cross
was the redemption of the world.

### America

Such miracles, unknown to us,
make me desire to believe;
but would the God that you reveal                      370

tan amorosa, que quiera
ofrecérseme en comida,
como Aquésta que yo adoro?

### Religión

Sí, pues Su Sabiduría,
para ese fin solamente,
entre los hombres habita.

### América

¿Y no veré yo a ese Dios,
para quedar convencida,

### Occidente

y para que de una vez
de mi tema me desista? 380

### Religión

Sí verás, como te laves
en la fuente cristalina
del Bautismo.

### Occidente

Ya yo sé
que antes que llegue a la rica
mesa, tengo de lavarme,
que así es mi costumbre antigua.

### Celo

No es aquése el lavatorio
que tus manchas necesitan.

### Occidente

¿Pues cuál?

### Religión

El de un Sacramento
que con virtud de aguas vivas 390
te limpie de tus pecados.

### América

Como me das las noticias
tan por mayor, no te acabo

offer Himself so lovingly
transformed for me into a meal
as does the god that I adore?

### Religion

In truth, He does. For this alone
His Wisdom came upon the earth
to dwell among all humankind.

### America

And so that I can be convinced,
may I not see this Deity?

### Occident

And so that I can be made free
of old beliefs that shackle me?                          380

### Religion

Yes, you will see when you are bathed
in crystal waters from the font
of baptism.

### Occident

       And well I know,
in preparation to attend
a banquet, I must bathe, or else
our ancient custom I offend.

### Zeal

Your vain ablutions will not do
the cleansing that your stains require.

### Occident

Then what?

### Religion

       There is a sacrament
of living waters, which can cleanse                       390
and purify you of your sins.

### America

Because you deluge my poor mind
with concepts of theology,

de entender; y así, querría
recibirlas por extenso,
pues ya inspiración divina
me mueve a querer saberlas.

### Occidente

Y yo; y más, saber la vida
y muerte de ese gran Dios
que estar en el Pan afirmas.                    400

### Religión

Pues vamos. Que en una idea
metafórica, vestida
de retóricos colores,
representable a tu vista,
te la mostraré; que ya
conozco que tú te inclinas
a objetos visibles, más
que a lo que la Fe te avisa
por el oído; y así,
es preciso que te sirvas                         410
de los ojos, para que
por ellos la Fe recibas.

### Occidente

Así es; que más quiero verlo,
que no que tú me lo digas.

---

## Escena V

### Religión

Vamos, pues.

### Celo

Religión, díme:
¿en qué forma determinas
representar los Misterios?

I've just begun to understand;
there is much more I want to see,
and my desire to know is now
by holy inspiration led.

### Occident

And I desire more keenly still
to know about the life and death
of the God you say is in the bread.                    400

### Religion

Then come along with me, and I
shall make for you a metaphor,
a concept clothed in rhetoric
so colorful that what I show
to you, your eyes will clearly see;
for now I know that you require
objects of sight instead of words,
by which faith whispers in your ears
too deaf to hear; I understand,
for you necessity demands                              410
that through the eyes, faith find her way
to her reception in your hearts.

### Occident

Exactly so.  I do prefer
to see the things you would impart.

---

# Scene 5

### Religion

Then come.

### Zeal

Religion, answer me:
what metaphor will you employ
to represent these mysteries?

### Religión

De un Auto en la alegoría,
quiero mostrarlos visibles,
para que quede instruída                    420
ella, y todo el Occidente,
de lo que ya solicita
saber.

### Celo

　¿Y cómo intitulas
el Auto que alegorizas?

### Religión

*Divino Narciso*, porque
si aquesta infeliz tenía
un Ídolo, que adoraba,
de tan extrañas divisas,
en quien pretendió el demonio,
de la Sacra Eucaristía                      430
fingir el alto Misterio,
sepa que también había
entre otros Gentiles, señas
de tan alta Maravilla.

### Celo

¿Y dónde se representa?

### Religión

En la coronada Villa
de Madrid, que es de la Fe
el Centro, y la Regia Silla
de sus Católicos Reyes,
a quien debieron las Indias                 440
las luces del Evangelio
que en el Occidente brillan.

### Celo

¿Pues no ves la impropiedad
de que en Méjico se escriba
y en Madrid se represente?

### Religion

An *auto* will make visible
through allegory images
of what America must learn                    420
and Occident implores to know
about the questions that now burn
within him so.

### Zeal

                    What will you call
this play in allegory cast?

### Religion

*Divine Narcissus*, let it be,
because if that unhappy maid
adored an idol which disguised
in such strange symbols the attempt
the demon made to counterfeit
the great and lofty mystery                   430
of the most Blessed Eucharist,
then there were also, I surmise,
among more ancient pagans hints
of such high marvels symbolized.

### Zeal

Where will your drama be performed?

### Religion

In the crown city of Madrid,
which is the center of the Faith,
the seat of Catholic majesty,
to whom the Indies owe their best
beneficence, the blessed gift                 440
of Holy Writ, the Gospel light
illuminating all the West.

### Zeal

That you should write in Mexico
for royal patrons don't you see
to be an impropriety?

### Religión

¿Pues es cosa nunca vista
que se haga una cosa en una
parte, porque en otra sirva?
Demás de que el escribirlo
no fué idea antojadiza,                                    450
sino debida obediencia
que aun a lo imposible aspira.
Con que su obra, aunque sea
rústica y poco pulida,
de la obediencia es efecto,
no parto de la osadía.

### Celo

Pues díme, Religión, ya
que a eso le diste salida,
¿cómo salvas la objeción
de que introduces las Indias,                             460
y a Madrid quieres llevarlas?

### Religión

Como aquesto sólo mira
a celebrar el Misterio,
y aquestas introducidas
personas no son más que
unos abstractos, que pintan
lo que se intenta decir,
no habrá cosa que desdiga,
aunque las lleve a Madrid:
que a especies intelectivas                               470
ni habrá distancias que estorben
ni mares que les impidan.

### Celo

Siendo así, a los Reales Pies,
en quien Dos Mundos se cifran,
pidamos perdón postrados;

### Religión

y a su Reina esclarecida,

### Religion

Is it beyond imagination
that something made in one location
can in another be of use?
Furthermore, my writing it
comes, not of whimsical caprice,               450
but from my vowed obedience
to do what seems beyond my reach.
Well, then, this work, however rough
and little polished it might be,
results from my obedience,
and not from any arrogance.

### Zeal

Then answer me, Religion, how
(before you leave the matter now),
will you respond when you are chid
for loading the whole Indies on               460
a stage to transport to Madrid?

### Religion

The purpose of my play can be
none other than to glorify
the Eucharistic Mystery;
and since the cast of characters
are no more than abstractions which
depict the theme with clarity,
then surely no one should object
if they are taken to Madrid;
distance can never hinder thought             470
with persons of intelligence,
nor seas impede exchange of sense.

### Zeal

Then, prostrate at his royal feet,
beneath whose strength two worlds are joined
we beg for pardon of the King;

### Religion

and from her eminence, the Queen;

*América*

cuyas soberanas plantas
besan humildes las Indias;

*Celo*

a sus Supremos Consejos;

*Religión*

a las Damas, que iluminan                                480
su Hemisferio;

*América*

     a sus Ingenios,
a quien humilde suplica
el mío, que le perdonen
el querer con toscas líneas
describir tanto Misterio.

*Occidente*

¡Vamos, que ya mi agonía
quiere ver cómo es el Dios
que me han de dar en comida,

(Cantan la América y el Occidente y el Celo:)

diciendo que ya
conocen las Indias
al que el Verdadero                                490
Dios de las Semillas!
Y en lágrimas tiernas
que el gozo destila,
repitan alegres
con voces festivas:

*Todos*

¡Dichoso el día
que conocí al gran Dios de las Semillas!


(Éntranse bailando y cantando.)

*America*

whose sovereign and anointed feet
the humble Indies bow to kiss;

*Zeal*

and from the Royal High Council;

*Religion*

and from the ladies, who bring light                    480
into their hemisphere;

*America*

        and from
their poets, I most humbly beg
forgiveness for my crude attempt,
desiring with these awkward lines
to represent the Mystery.

*Occident*

Let's go, for anxiously I long to see
exactly how this God of yours
will give Himself as food to me.

(America, Occident, and Zeal sing:)

The Indies know
and do concede
who is the true                                          490
God of the Seeds.
In loving tears
which joy prolongs
we gladly sing
our happy songs.

*All*

Blest be the day
when I could see
and worship the
great God of Seeds.                                      500

(They all exit, dancing and singing.)

# Auto Sacramental *de*
# El Divino Narciso

PERSONAS QUE HABLAN EN ÉL

El Divino Narciso
La Gracia
La Gentilidad
La Sinagoga
La Naturaleza Humana
Eco, que hace La Naturaleza
  Angélica (Réproba)

Dos Coros de Música
La Soberbia
El Amor Propio
Ninfas y Pastores

---

## ESCENA I

(Salen, por una parte, la Gentilidad, de Ninfa, con acompañamiento de Ninfas y Pastores; y por otra, la Sinagoga, también de
Ninfa, con su acompañamiento, que serán los Músicos; y detrás,
muy bizarra, la Naturaleza Humana, oyendo lo que cantan.)

*Sinagoga*

¡Alabad al Señor todos los Hombres!

*Coro 1*

¡Alabad al Señor todos los Hombres!

*Sinagoga*

Un nuevo canto entonad
a Su divina Beldad
y en cuanto la luz alcanza,
suene la eterna alabanza
de la gloria de Su nombre.

*Coro 1*

¡Alabad al Señor todos los Hombres!

*Gentilidad*

¡Aplaudid a Narciso, Fuentes y Flores!

# *Auto Sacramental*
# The Divine Narcissus

The Divine Narcissus      Two Choral Groups
Grace      Pride
Gentile      Self-Love
Synagogue      Nymphs and Shepherds
Human Nature
Echo, who plays the part of Angelic
    Nature, fallen from grace

---

## SCENE 1

(Enter on one side, Gentile, dressed as a nymph and accompanied
by nymphs and shepherds; on the other side, Synagogue, also
dressed as a nymph and accompanied by musicians. Behind them
is Human Nature, looking on with curiosity and listening to
what they are singing.)

*Synagogue*

All you peoples, praise the Lord!

*First Chorus*

All you peoples, praise the Lord!

*Synagogue*

Sing a new song unto the Lord,
Sing to His loveliness divine
and for as long as light will shine,
may you eternal praise accord
unto the glory of His name.

*First Chorus*

All you peoples, praise the Lord!

*Gentile*

You fountains and you flowers, praise

Y pues su beldad divina,
sin igualdad peregrina,
es sobre toda hermosura
que se vió en otra criatura,
y en todas inspira amores,

*Coro 2*

¡alabad a Narciso, Fuentes y Flores!

*Sinagoga*

¡Alabad,

*Gentilidad*

aplaudid,

*Sinagoga*

con himnos,

*Gentilidad*

con voces,

*Sinagoga*

al Señor,

*Gentilidad*

a Narciso

*Sinagoga*

todos los Hombres,

*Gentilidad*

Fuentes y Flores!

(Pónese la Naturaleza Humana en medio de los dos Coros)

*Naturaleza Humana*

Gentilidad, Sinagoga,
que en dulces métricas voces
a Dios aplaude la una,                           20
y la otra celebra a un Hombre:

Narcissus! His divinity
in beauty walks without compare,
and since his beauty is so rare,
surpassing that of creatures, he
inspires love in all who gaze.

*Second Chorus*

Fountains, flowers, praise Narcissus!

*Synagogue*

Praise,

*Gentile*

applaud,

*Synagogue*

with hymns,

*Gentile*

with voices,

*Synagogue*

the Lord,

*Gentile*

Narcissus,

*Synagogue*

all you peoples,

*Gentile*

fountains! flowers!

(Human Nature steps forward and stands between the two choral groups.)

*Human Nature*

O Gentile child and Synagogue,
who sing in voices sweetly measured,
(the one gives praise unto her God;                          20
the other celebrates a man):

escuchadme lo que os digo,
atended a mis razones,
que pues soy Madre de entrambas,
a entrambas es bien que toque
por ley natural oírme.

### Sinagoga

Ya mi amor te reconoce,
oh Naturaleza, Madre
común de todos los hombres.

### Gentilidad

Y yo también te obedezco,                    30
pues aunque andemos discordes
yo y la Sinagoga, no
por eso te desconoce
mi amor, antes te venera.

### Sinagoga

Y sólo en esto conformes
estamos, pues observamos,
ella allá entre sus errores
y yo acá entre mis verdades,
aquel precepto, que impone,
de que uno a otro no le haga          40
lo que él para sí no abone;
y como Padre ninguno
quiere que el hijo le enoje,
así no fuera razón
que a nuestras obligaciones
faltáramos, con negar
nuestra atención a tus voces.

### Gentilidad

Así es; porque este precepto,
porque ninguno lo ignore,
se lo escribes a tus hijos
dentro de los corazones.          50

### Naturaleza Humana

Bien está; que ese precepto,
basta, para que se note

now let my words enter your ears,
and in your hearts let them be treasured.
Since I am mother to you both,
in each, let Natural Law inspire
the listening you yourselves desire.

### Synagogue

My heart already knows you well,
declaring you, oh Nature, as
the common mother of us all.

### Gentile

And I obey you even though                    30
my sister Synagogue and I
may walk in disagreement; know
that still my love acknowledges
you, Mother, bowing down to you.

### Synagogue

On one side she, with her heresy,
on the other I, with my truth held high,
in this alone find unity:
we both observe most carefully
that precept which demands that we
will do to others nothing that              40
we do not wish done to ourselves;
and even as no father will
wish his son to anger him,
neither was it our intent
to fail to pay our lawful debt
and wake your wrath, denying to
your words our filial respect.

### Gentile

And that is true, because this law
is one no person may ignore,
for you have written it upon              50
the hearts of all your family.

### Human Nature

How glad I am to know this law
convinces you to render me

que como a Madre común
me debéis las atenciones.

*Sinagoga*

Pues dínos lo que pretendes.

*Gentilidad*

Pues dínos lo que dispones.

*Naturaleza Humana*

Digo, que habiendo escuchado
en vuestras métricas voces
los diferentes objetos
de vuestras aclamaciones:                          60
pues tú, Gentilidad ciega,
errada, ignorante y torpe,
a una caduca beldad
aplaudes en tus loores,
y tú, Sinagoga, cierta
de las verdades que oyes
en tus Profetas, a Dios
Le rindes veneraciones;
dejando de discurrir                               70
en vuestras oposiciones,
pues claro está que tú yerras

(A la Gentilidad)

y claro el que tú conoces,

(A la Sinagoga)

aunque vendrá tiempo, en que
trocándose las acciones,
la Gentilidad conozca,
y la Sinagoga ignore . . .
Mas esto ahora no es del caso;
y así, volviéndome al orden
del discurso, digo que                             80
oyendo vuestras canciones,
me he pasado a cotejar
cuán misteriosas se esconden
aquellas ciertas verdades
debajo de estas ficciones.

as mother to all humankind
the same attention you desire.

### Synagogue

Then tell us what it is you wish.

### Gentile

Reveal what you resolve to do.

### Human Nature

Then I reply that I have heard
in your poetic songs of praise
how different are the objects of                    60
the acclamations that you raise:
for you, Gentile, but blindly gaze,
mistaken, ignorant, and dull,
applauding a dead beauty
in your paean's every phrase.
And, Synagogue, sure of the truth
which you hear in the Prophets, you
listen and respond, and thus,
give praise to God, living and true.
Now we can leave the topic of                       70
the oppositions which you pose,

(To Gentile)

since clearly you are much mistaken,

(To Synagogue)

and clearly it is you who knows,
and yet a time will come in which
your situation will transpose
and Gentile be the one who knows
while Synagogue be ignorant,
but that eventuality
remains yet to be seen.
And now, returning to the point,                    80
I say that I have heard your songs,
and I do not distinguish when
these mysteries appear dressed in
the cloak of truth and when they screen
themselves behind the veil of myth.

Pues si en tu Narciso, tú
tanta perfección supones,
que dices que es su hermosura
imán de los corazones,
y que no sólo la siguen                    90
las Ninfas y los Pastores,
sino las aves y fieras,
los collados y los montes,
los arroyos y las fuentes,
las plantas, hierbas y flores,
¿con cuánta mayor razón
estas sumas perfecciones
se verifican de Dios,
a cuya Beldad, los Orbes,
para servirle de espejos,                 100
indignos se reconocen;
y a Quien todas las criaturas
(aunque no hubiera razones
de tan grandes beneficios,
de tan extraños favores)
por Su Hermosura, no más,
debieran adoraciones;
y a Quien la Naturaleza
(que soy yo), con atenciones,
como a mi Centro apetezco                 110
y sigo como a mi Norte?
Y así, pues Madre de entrambas
soy, intento con colores
alegóricos, que ideas
representables componen

(A la Sinagoga)

    tomar de la una el sentido,

(A la Gentilidad)

    tomar de la otra las voces,
y en metafóricas frases,
tomando sus locuciones
y en figura de Narciso,                   120
solicitar los amores
de Dios, a ver si dibujan
estos obscuros borrones
la claridad de Sus luces;

Then if, in your Narcissus, you
such great perfection presuppose;
if as a magnet he attracts
all hearts to him as you disclose;
and if, not only nature's nymphs                    90
and shepherd girls alike suppose
his beauty irresistible
and follow him; but birds and beasts,
hills and mountains, streams and fountains,
herbs and grasses, even the rose;
then must there not be greater cause
for such perfections to reveal
their presence in our Deity,
before whose beauty crystalline
celestial spheres discover their                    100
unworthiness to mirror Him?
To Him all creatures of the earth
(to whom He gives such benefits
and without reason rains upon them
such extraordinary favors)
owe their profound adoration
and to his beauty, veneration.
It is to Him that I myself,
great Nature, gravitate as if
He were my very center point                         110
and follow Him as my lodestar.
Since I am mother to you both,
then both will further my intent:
that allegory's palette lend
to truth color and clarity;

(To Synagogue)

      from one, the meaning I shall take,

(To Gentile)

and from the other, I take words,
and from the figure of Narcissus,
I take his speeches, reading them
as metaphors which represent                         120
the love of God, to see if these
dark sketches can be made to trace
the outlines and the clarity
of God's illuminated face;

pues muchas veces conformes
Divinas y Humanas Letras,
dan a entender que Dios pone
aun en las Plumas Gentiles
unos visos en que asomen
los altos Misterios Suyos;                    130
y así quiero que, concordes,
tú des el cuerpo a la idea,

(A la Sinagoga)

y tú el vestido le cortes.

(A la Gentilidad)

¿Qué decís?

### Sinagoga

Que por la parte
que del intento me toque,
te serviré yo con darte
en todo lo que te importen,
los versos de mis Profetas,
los coros de mis Cantores.

### Gentilidad

Yo, aunque no te entiendo bien,         140
pues es lo que me propones,
que sólo te dé materia
para que tú allá la informes
de otra alma, de otro sentido
que mis ojos no conocen,
te daré de humanas letras
los poéticos primores
de la historia de Narciso.

### Naturaleza Humana

Pues volved a las acordes
músicas, en que os hallé,                    150
porque quien oyere, logre
en la metáfora el ver
que, en estas amantes voces,
una cosa es la que entiende
y otra cosa la que oye.

it oft falls out that Holy Writ,
with human poetry agrees,
and they reveal that God has placed
in even Gentile pens the pow'r
of images that flicker light
upon His lofty mysteries;                              130
and thus, I wish, with your assent,

(To Synagogue)

        that you give body to the thought,

(To Gentile)

        and you, to dress it, cut the cloth.
        Do you consent?

### Synagogue

        Whatever task
may fall to me, I gladly take;
whatever treasure you may ask
to fit your purpose, I shall make
a gift—my cantors' sacred songs,
the verses of my prophets' speech.

### Gentile

Although I do not understand                           140
the project you propose, still I
will gladly give the language and
the form, for which you will devise
another soul, another sense
that my eyes cannot recognize.
From human letters I will bring
poetic elegance that sings
the story of Narcissus' fate.

### Human Nature

Return, then, to the harmony
in which I found you singing, for                       150
whoever hears these loving words
may gain from them the power to see
what lies behind the metaphor;
for hearing words is not the same
as understanding mystery.

# *Auto Sacramental de*
# El Divino Narciso

Personas que hablan en él

El Divino Narciso
La Gracia
La Gentilidad
La Sinagoga
La Naturaleza Humana
Eco, que hace La Naturaleza
    Angélica (Réproba)

Dos Coros de Música
La Soberbia
El Amor Propio
Ninfas y Pastores

---

## Escena I

(Salen, por una parte, la Gentilidad, de Ninfa, con acompañamiento de Ninfas y Pastores; y por otra, la Sinagoga, también de
Ninfa, con su acompañamiento, que serán los Músicos; y detrás,
muy bizarra, la Naturaleza Humana, oyendo lo que cantan.)

*Sinagoga*

¡Alabad al Señor todos los Hombres!

*Coro 1*

¡Alabad al Señor todos los Hombres!

*Sinagoga*

Un nuevo canto entonad
a Su divina Beldad
y en cuanto la luz alcanza,
suene la eterna alabanza
de la gloria de Su nombre.

*Coro 1*

¡Alabad al Señor todos los Hombres!

*Gentilidad*

¡Aplaudid a Narciso, Fuentes y Flores!

# *Auto Sacramental*
# The Divine Narcissus

SPEAKING CHARACTERS

The Divine Narcissus     Two Choral Groups
Grace     Pride
Gentile     Self-Love
Synagogue     Nymphs and Shepherds
Human Nature
Echo, who plays the part of Angelic
   Nature, fallen from grace

---

## SCENE 1

(Enter on one side, Gentile, dressed as a nymph and accompanied by nymphs and shepherds; on the other side, Synagogue, also dressed as a nymph and accompanied by musicians. Behind them is Human Nature, looking on with curiosity and listening to what they are singing.)

*Synagogue*

All you peoples, praise the Lord!

*First Chorus*

All you peoples, praise the Lord!

*Synagogue*

Sing a new song unto the Lord,
Sing to His loveliness divine
and for as long as light will shine,
may you eternal praise accord
unto the glory of His name.

*First Chorus*

All you peoples, praise the Lord!

*Gentile*

You fountains and you flowers, praise

## Escena II

*Sinagoga*

¡Alabad al Señor todos los Hombres!

*Coro 1*

¡Alabad al Señor todos los Hombres!

*Gentilidad*

¡Aplaudid a Narciso, Fuentes y Flores!

*Coro 2*

¡Aplaudid a Narciso, Fuentes y Flores!

*Sinagoga*

Todos los Hombres Le alaben                    160
y nunca su aplauso acaben
los Ángeles en su altura,
el Cielo con su hermosura,
y con sus giros los Orbes.

*Coro 1*

¡Alabad al Señor todos los Hombres!

*Coro 2*

¡Aplaudid a Narciso, Fuentes y Flores!

*Gentilidad*

Y pues Su beldad hermosa,
soberana y prodigiosa,
es de todas la mayor,
cuyo sin igual primor                          170
aplauden los horizontes,

*Coro 2*

¡aplaudid a Narciso, Fuentes y Flores!

*Coro 1*

¡Alabad al Señor todos los Hombres!

# Scene 2

*Synagogue*

All you peoples, praise the Lord!

*First Chorus*

All you peoples, praise the Lord!

*Gentile*

Fountains, flowers, praise Narcissus!

*Second Chorus*

Fountains, flowers, praise Narcissus!

*Synagogue*

Let all the peoples give Him praise,        160
and may the angels throned on high
not cease to sing and glorify
with the beauty of the heavens
and the turning of the spheres.

*First Chorus*

All you peoples, praise the Lord!

*Second Chorus*

Applaud Narcissus, founts and flowers!

*Gentile*

And since His beauty is sublime,
so sovereign and marvelous
that it excels in space and time,
let horizons sing and praise        170
His excellence through endless days.

*Second Chorus*

Applaud Narcissus, founts and flowers!

*First Chorus*

All you peoples, praise the Lord!

### Sinagoga

Las Aguas que sobre el Cielo
forman cristalino hielo,
y las excelsas Virtudes
que moran sus celsitudes,
todas Le alaben conformes.

### Coro 1

¡Alabad al Señor todos los Hombres!

### Coro 2

¡Aplaudid a Narciso, Fuentes y Flores!                    180

### Gentilidad

A su bello resplandor
se para el claro Farol
del Sol; y por ver Su Cara,
el fogoso carro para,
mirando sus perfecciones.

### Coro 2

¡Aplaudid a Narciso, Fuentes y Flores!

### Coro 1

¡Alabad al Señor todos los Hombres!

### Sinagoga

El Sol, la Luna y Estrellas,
el Fuego con sus centellas,
la Niebla con el Rocío.                                   190
la Nieve, el Hielo y el Frío
y los Días y las Noches.

### Coro 1

¡Alabad al Señor todos los Hombres!

### Coro 2

¡Aplaudid a Narciso, Fuentes y Flores!

### Gentilidad

Su atractivo singular
no sólo llega a arrastrar

*Synagogue*

All waters high above the heavens
that crystallize to sparkling ice,
and the lofty choir of angels,
inhabiting celestial heights,
all together, praise the Lord.

*First Chorus*

All you peoples, praise the Lord!

*Second Chorus*

Applaud Narcissus, founts and flowers!                    180

*Gentile*

The golden lantern of the sun
its radiance and beauty dims;
its chariots of fire run
no more, standing in awe of him,
wondering at his perfections.

*Second Chorus*

Applaud Narcissus, founts and flowers!

*First Chorus*

All you peoples, praise the Lord!

*Synagogue*

Bright sun and moon and twinkling stars,
fiery blaze with sparks that flare,
misty vapors, sprinkling dew,                             190
snow and ice and frigid air,
swift-footed Day and limping Night.

*First Chorus*

All you peoples, praise the Lord!

*Second Chorus*

Applaud Narcissus, founts and flowers!

*Gentile*

His singular attractiveness
draws to him irresistibly

las Ninfas y los Zagales,
en su seguimiento iguales,
mas las Peñas y los Montes.

*Coro 2*

¡Aplaudid a Narciso, Fuentes y Flores!               200

*Coro 1*

¡Alabad al Señor, todos los Hombres!

*Naturaleza Humana*

¡Oh, qué bien suenan unidas
las alabanzas acordes,
que de Su Beldad divina
celebran las perfecciones!
Que aunque las desdichas mías
desterrada de Sus soles
me tienen, no me prohiben
el que Su Belleza adore;
que aunque, justamente airado               210
por mis delitos enormes,
me desdeña, no me faltan
piadosos intercesores
que Le insten continuamente
para que el perdón me otorgue,
y el estar en mí Su imagen,
bien que los raudales torpes
de las aguas de mis culpas
toda mi belleza borren:
que a las culpas, el Sagrado               220
Texto, en muchas ocasiones
aguas llama, cuando dice:
"No la tempestad me ahogue
del agua"; y en otra parte,
alabando los favores
de Dios, repite David
que su Dios, que le socorre,
le libró de muchas aguas;
y que los intercesores
llegan en tiempo oportuno,               230
pero que no en los furores
del diluvio de las aguas.
Y así, bien es que yo nombre

not only nymph and shepherdess,
but woodlands with each kind of tree,
and rocks pursuing him no less.

*Second Chorus*

Applaud Narcissus, founts and flowers!                    200

*First Chorus*

All you peoples, praise the Lord!

*Human Nature*

How wondrous is the harmony
of praises sung in one accord,
to celebrate epiphanies
of beauty, in Him made divine!
Although my sinful indigence
has banished me far from His sight,
no law prevents my worshipping
His beauty in my heart's own shrine
and even though, so justly wroth                          210
because of my enormous sins,
He may reject me, yet I have
most pious intercessors who
pray to Him continually
to pardon me, and I possess
within my soul the image
of His face, although the swift
and constant torrent of my faults
erodes my beauty day by day:
the Sacred Scriptures frequently,                         220
in many well-known passages,
call these faults "waters," when they say:
"Let not the floodwaters drown me,"
and in another place is told
how David did continually
give praise for his deliverance
from waters deep and dangerous;
through his God's great benignity;
he prayed for intercessors
to come at the propitious hour,                           230
but that their coming would not be
during the raging of the flood.
And for these reasons do I call

aguas turbias a mi culpa,
cuyos obscenos colores
entre mí y Él interpuestos,
tanto mi sér descomponen,
tanto mi belleza afean,
tanto alteran mis facciones,
que si las mira Narciso,          240
a Su imagen desconoce.
Díganlo, después de aquel
pecado del primer hombre,
que fué mar, cuyas espumas
no hay ninguno que no mojen,
tántas fuentes, tántos ríos
obscenos de pecadores,
en quien la Naturaleza
siempre sumergida, esconde
Su hermosura. ¡Oh, quiera el Cielo      250
que mis esperanzas topen
alguna Fuente que, libre
de aquellas aguas salobres,
represente de Narciso
enteras las perfecciones!
Y mientras quiere mi dicha
que yo sus cristales toque,
vosotros, para ablandar
de Narciso los rigores,
repetid sus alabanzas          260
en tiernas aclamaciones,
uniendo a cláusulas llanto,
porque es lo mejor que oye.
Representad mi dolor;
que vuestras voces acordes
puede ser que Lo enternezcan,
y piadoso me perdone.
Y pues en edad ninguna
ha faltado quien abogue
por mí, vamos a buscar          270
la Fuente en que mis borrones
se han de lavar, sin dejar
las dulces repeticiones
de la Música, diciendo
entre lágrimas y voces:

my evil muddy waters too,
whose darkly-colored murkiness
so separates my Love from me,
so much disintegrates my soul,
so much disfigures my beauty,
so alters my lineaments,
that my Narcissus, seeing them,        240
could not discern His image there.
Then, let the tragic tale be told
how after our first father's sin,
which was a sea, whose filthy foam
contaminated everyone,
so many fountains, many streams,
and rivers were polluted,
sinners in whom Nature hides,
her loveliness, always submerged.
Oh, would that heaven might vouchsafe      250
to grant my hope one day to find
some crystal fountain pure and free
of dark and muddy brackish waters,
to mirror in its clear reflections
Narcissus' absolute perfections!
My happiness depends upon
my touching it, and until then,
to soften His severity,
I implore that you, my daughters,
repeat the praises of Narcissus      260
by singing tender acclamations
and punctuating words with tears,
for this, He most desires to hear.
Express so well my misery
that by your voices' sweet accord,
He might be moved to pity me
and offer pardon graciously.
And since I have not ever lacked
in any age an advocate
to intercede for me, let us      270
seek out this fountain presently,
in which my sins have to be cleansed,
and do not cease your repetition
of the music, sweetly praying
with your voices and your tears:

*Coro 1*

¡Alabad al señor todos los Hombres!

*Coro 2*

¡Aplaudid a Narciso, Fuentes y Flores!

---

## Escena III

(Éntranse, y salen Eco, Ninfa, alborotada; la Soberbia, de Pastora;
el Amor Propio, de Pastor.)

*Eco*

Soberbia, Amor Propio, amigos,
¿oísteis en esta selva
unas voces?

*Soberbia*

      Yo atendí                                   280
sus cláusulas; por más señas,
que mucho más que el oído,
el corazón me penetran.

*Amor Propio*

Yo también, que al escuchar
lo dulce de sus cadencias,
fuera de mi acuerdo estoy.

*Eco*

Pues, y bien, ¿qué inferís de ellas?

*Soberbia*

Nada, porque sólo yo
conozco que me molestan,
como la Soberbia soy,                                   290
las alabanzas ajenas.

*Amor Propio*

Yo sólo sé que me cansan
cariños que se enderezan

*First Chorus*

All you peoples, praise the Lord!

*Second Chorus*

Applaud Narcissus, founts and flowers!

---

## SCENE 3

(Enter [Satan, who will appear as] Echo, a nymph, greatly agitated; Pride, a shepherd girl; and Self-Love, a Shepherd boy.)

*Echo [Satan]*

Self-Love and Pride, my faithful friends,
have you been hearing sounds like voices
in the forest?

*Pride*

    I have listened                    280
to their discourse, and more than words
have touched my ears; both sound and sense
have penetrated to my heart.

*Self-Love*

And I as well, from listening
to the sweetness of their rhythms,
am awestruck and beside myself.

*Echo [Satan]*

Well, then, what do you make of this?

*Pride*

Nothing at all, for I alone,
since I am Pride, can understand
how these exotic praises can          290
my satisfaction countermand.

*Self-Love*

And only I can know, because
I am Self-Love, how it can irk

como yo soy Amor Propio,
a amar a quien yo no sea.

*Eco*

Pues yo os diré lo que infiero,
que como mi infusa ciencia
se distingue de mi Propio
Amor, y de mi Soberbia,
no es mucho que no la alcancen,                    300
y es natural que la teman.
Y así, Amor Propio, que en mí
tan inseparable reinas,
que haces que de mí me olvide,
por hacer que a mí me quiera
(porque el Amor Propio
es de tal manera,
que insensato olvida
lo mismo que acuerda);
Principio de mis afectos,                          310
pues eres en quien empiezan,
y tú eres en quien acaban,
pues acaban en Soberbia
(porque cuando el Amor Propio
de lo que es razón se aleja,
en Soberbia se remata,
que es el afecto que engendra,
que es aquel que todas
las cosas intenta
sólo dirigidas                                     320
a su conveniencia),
escuchadme. Ya habéis visto
que aquesta Pastora bella
representa en común toda
la Humana Naturaleza:
que en figura de una Ninfa,
con metafórica idea,
sigue a una Beldad que adora,
no obstante que la desprecia;
y para que a las Divinas                           330
sirvan las Humanas Letras,
valiéndose de las dos,
su conformidad coteja,
tomando a unas el sentido,

to find an object of affection
outside the self—what weary work!

*Echo [Satan]*

Then I shall tell you what I think:
since my infused intelligence
so well distinguishes herself
from my Self-Love and from my Pride
who are so far inferior,                                    300
they naturally are terrified.
And so, Self-Love, the one in me
who governs so inseparably,
makes me forget just who I am
so he can make me love myself,
[Aside] (because the nature of Self-Love
is that he foolishly forgets
his true self, but remembers well
the false self that the mind begets);
origin of my affections                                    310
which start in you, in you abide,
in you they end, and in the end,
are metamorphosed into Pride
[Aside] (because when Self-Love moves away
from what is rational and right,
then he transforms himself to Pride,
which is the principal emotion
that Self-Love can arouse, the one
which every single thing will guide
in the direction of her will                               320
as her convenience may decide.)
Now listen. You already know
that this lovely shepherdess
stands for the commonality
of Human Nature; and that she,
clad in the costume of a nymph,
(I now speak metaphorically),
pursues a beauty she adores,
who nonetheless despises her;
and so that human poetry                                   330
might minister to Holy Writ,
she takes some elements from both,
combining them where they agree,
abstracting meaning from the one,

y a las otras la corteza,
y prosiguiendo las frases,
usando de la licencia
de retóricos colores,
que son uno, y otro muestran,
Narciso a Dios llama,         340
porque Su Belleza
no habrá quien la iguale,
ni quien la merezca.
Pues ahora, puesto que
mi persona representa
el Sér Angélico, no
en común, mas sólo aquella
parte réproba, que osada
arrastró de las Estrellas
la tercer parte al Abismo,         350
quiero, siguiendo la misma
metáfora que ella, hacer
a otra Ninfa; que pues ella
como una Ninfa a Narciso
sigue, ¿qué papel me queda
hacer, sino a Eco infeliz,
que de Narciso se queja?
Pues ¿qué más Beldad
que la Suya inmensa,
ni qué más desprecio         360
que el que a mí me muestra?
Y así, aunque ya lo sabéis,
por lo que a mí me atormenta
(que soy yo tal, que ni a mí
reservo la mayor pena),
os referiré la historia
con la metáfora misma,
para ver si la de Eco
conviene con mi tragedia.
Desde aquí el curioso         370
mire si concuerdan
verdad y ficción,
el sentido y letra.

and from the other taking form;
and with poetic license, she
composes sentences of such
iridescent rhetoric
that what they seem, they never mean;
therefore, she calls Narcissus God,       340
because His beauty far exceeds
all others, and there is no one
who can deserve or equal it.
Now I am placed in that same plot,
and in my person represent
Angelic Nature, not entire,
but that part whose rebellion bars
its bliss, the dissolute and damned,
whose daring dragged to the Abyss
a third part of the weeping stars;       350
and following a metaphor
identical to hers, I want
to fashion yet another nymph,
who follows her Narcissus, for
whatever role could I play now
but an unhappy Echo who
laments Narcissus constantly?
That being so, what can surpass
His beauty, which is so immense,
and what surpasses anywhere       360
His scorn of me, deep and intense?
And though you may already guess
my story from how I complain,
(it is not in my nature to
save for myself the greatest pain),
still I will tell it to you now,
using the self-same metaphor
so you can judge if Echo's tale
echoes the tale I told before.
From that, the curious might reflect       370
upon the possible accord
between these fictions and the truth,
between significance and word.

[Satan pulls on a dress and a wig and steps forward to play the part of Echo.]

Ya sabéis que yo soy Eco,
la que infelizmente bella,
por querer ser más hermosa
me reduje a ser más fea,
porque—viéndome dotada
de hermosura y de nobleza,
de valor y de virtud, 380
de perfección y de ciencia,
y en fin, viendo que era yo,
aun de la Naturaleza
Angélica ilustre mía,
la criatura más perfecta—,
ser esposa de Narciso
quise, e intenté soberbia
poner mi asiento en Su Solio
e igualarme a su grandeza,
juzgando que no 390
era inconsecuencia
que fuera igual Suya
quien era tan bella;
por lo cual, Él, ofendido,
tan desdeñoso me deja,
tan colérico me arroja
de Su gracia y Su presencia,
que no me dejó ¡ay de mí!,
esperanza de que pueda
volver a gozar los rayos 400
de Su Divina Belleza.
Yo, viéndome despreciada,
con el dolor de mi afrenta,
en odio trueco el amor
y en rencores la terneza,
en venganzas los cariños,
y cual víbora sangrienta,
nociva ponzoña exhalo,
veneno animan mis venas;
que cuando el amor 410
en odio se trueca,
es más eficaz
el rencor que engendra.
Y temerosa de que
la Humana Naturaleza

I am called Echo, as you know,
unhappily so beautiful,
who wished that beauty greater grow
and was reduced to ugliness,
because—I saw myself blessed so
with beauty and nobility,
with courage and with virtue's strength,          380
perfection's height and wisdom's breadth,
and understanding well, at length,
that I, among celestial peers,
who of angelic nature are,
exceeded them, a perfect star—
I wished to be Narcissus' spouse,
and I intended, in my pride,
to be enthroned at His right side,
to share his grandeur equally;
I saw no inconsistency,          390
and it seemed logical to me
that I, who was so beautiful,
deserved to have equality.
Offended for this reason,
so disdainfully He leaves,
so angrily He casts me out
from His presence and His grace,
so that I had no hope, ay me!
no possibility to see
once more the beauty of His face,          400
which radiates divinity.
Reflecting on myself so scorned,
and saddened by the insult,
I twist affection into hate,
turn tenderness into a grudge,
exchange endearments for revenge,
and like a bloody viper,
I exhale a noxious poison
generated in my veins.
When love's denied          410
and turned to hate,
the rancor it spawns
will never abate.
And fearful, since I now could see
that Human Nature might perceive

los laureles que perdí,
venturosa se merezca,
inventé tales ardides,
formé tal estratagema,
que a la incauta Ninfa obligo, 420
sin atender mi cautela,
que a Narciso desobligue,
y que ingrata y desatenta
Le ofenda, viendo que Él es
de condición tan severa,
que ofendido ya una vez,
como es infinita ofensa
la que se hace a Su Deidad,
no hay medio para que vuelva
a Su gracia, porque 430
es tanta la deuda,
que nadie es capaz
de satisfacerla.
Y con esto a la infeliz
la reduje a tal miseria,
que por más que tristemente
gime al són de sus cadenas,
son en vano sus suspiros,
son inútiles sus quejas,
pues, como yo, no podrá 440
eternamente risueña
ver la cara de Narciso:
con lo cual vengada queda
mi injuria, porque
ya que no posea
yo el Solio, no es bien
que otra lo merezca,
ni que lo que yo perdí,
una villana grosera,
de tosco barro formada, 450
hecha de baja materia,
llegue a lograr. Así es bien
que estemos todos alerta,
para que nunca Narciso
a mirar sus ojos vuelva:
porque es a Él tan parecida,
en efecto, como hecha

herself deserving worthily
to take the laurels I had lost,
I then resorted to such wiles,
and planned such strategems, that soon
the nymph, devoid of any guile,                    420
and unaware of my intent
that she, discourteous and rude,
her lord Narcissus would offend,
she fell; her sin, ingratitude.
His disposition is severe,
and so austere that even one
small sin results in such a debt
that there is no way to return
to His good grace, because to sin
against His sovereign Deity                        430
results in consequences which
are infinite and cannot be
by any person satisfied.
And thus did I reduce the nymph
to such great depths of misery,
that she unhappily complains,
in chorus with her heavy chains;
but all her tearful sighs are vain,
and her laments have no effect,
because, like me, she will not be                  440
allowed to see Narcissus' face,
which smiles for all eternity;
and thus, at last, am I avenged
to compensate my injury,
for now since I can never have
the role of queen and royal chair,
that someone else be given all
that I have lost cannot be fair;
and that a gross and churlish peasant,
who's made of lowly stuff like dirt                450
and common clay, which is inert,
succeeds instead distresses me.
And thus, we must all be alert
so that Narcissus will not see
this lowly maid with His own eyes
because, in her appearance, she
resembles Him so much, in fact,

a Su imagen (¡ay de mí!,
de envidia el pecho revienta),
que temo que, si la mira,                          460
Su imagen que mira en ella
obligará a Su Deidad
a que se incline a quererla;
que la semejanza
tiene tanta fuerza,
que no puede haber
quien no la apetezca.
Y así, siempre he procurado
con cuidado y diligencia
borrar esta semejanza,                             470
haciéndola que cometa
tales pecados, que Él mismo
-soltando a Acuario las riendas-
destruyó por agua el mundo,
en venganza de su ofensa.


Mas como es costumbre Suya,
que siempre piadoso mezcla
en medio de la Justicia
los visos de la Clemencia,
quiso, no obstante el naufragio,                   480
que a favor de la primera
nadante tabla, salvase
la vida que aún hoy conserva;
que aun entre el enojo,
siempre se Le acuerda
la Misericordia,
para usar más de ella.
Pero apenas respiró
del daño, cuando Soberbia,
con homenajes altivos                              490
escalar el cielo intenta,
y creyendo su ignorancia
que era accesible la Esfera
a corporales fatigas
y a materiales tareas,

that she His image is. (Ay, me!
With envy now my heart is cracked!)
And if He sees her, I'm afraid                    460
His image which she mirrors back
will obligate His Deity
to yield Himself to loving her
because their similarity
is like a magnet of such strength,
so irresistible, that He
cannot be else but drawn to her.
And therefore I have always tried
with utmost diligence and care
to mar the likeness that they share          470
by tempting her to slip and slide
into such sins as those for which
He loosed the reins of Aquarius,
submerging the entire world
to punish it for her offence.

[Thunder and lightning. Behind Echo, a medieval cart containing
a small stage rolls out. On it are Noah's ark, the Tower of Babel,
and an idol.]

But since He customarily
is always merciful, then He
mixes with just severity
the soft luster of clemency;
however deadly the shipwreck          480
of sin, He sent without delay
the first life-boat, for He willed to save
and preserve life, as He does today;
thus, even in the midst of rage
He does forever call to mind
mercy's mitigating vision
to use it and be ever kind.
(She pauses in her tale, for pain
has nearly snatched away her breath.)
And then bold Pride, with haughty oaths,      490
attempts to stride to heaven's height,
believing, in his ignorance,
by braving bodily distress,
and doing great material tasks,
that to the spheres he'll gain access,

altiva Torre fabrica,
pudiendo labrar más cuerda
inmateriales escalas
hechas de su penitencia.
A cuya loca ambición, 500
en proporcionada pena,
correspondió en divisiones
la confusión de las lenguas;
que es justo castigo
al que necio piensa
que lo entiende todo,
que a ninguno entienda.
Después de así divididos,
les insistí a tales sectas,
que ya adoraban al Sol, 510
ya el curso de las Estrellas,
ya veneraban los brutos,
ya daban culto a las peñas,
ya a las fuentes, ya a los ríos,
ya a los bosques, ya a las selvas,
sin que quedara criatura,
por inmunda o por obscena,
que su ceguedad dejara,
que su ignorancia excluyera;
y adorando embelesados 520
sus inclinaciones mismas,
olvidaron de su Dios
la adoración verdadera;
conque amando Estatuas
su ignorancia ciega,
vinieron a casi
tranformarse en ellas.

so he erects a lofty tower,
thinking his project far more wise
than building immaterial stairs
of tears that stream from penitent eyes.
The punishment proportionate                           500
to his ambitious, mad illusion
has split our common mother tongue,
condemning speech to great confusion;
which, as a punishment to one
who thinks that he knows everything
and may, in fact, quite miss the mark,
the loss of speech is a just sting.
And thus, the languages divided,
I split religion into sects,
so that, for some the sun provided                     510
a god; for some, the distant stars;
while some adored ferocious beasts;
still others worshiped the high mountains,
the flowing rivers and the fountains,
and trees in jungles, forests green;
and soon there was no creature which,
however filthy and obscene,
their blindness would not leave alone,
nor their great ignorance exclude,
and, adoring fascinations                               520
made in their imaginations,
they lost remembrance of their God,
the object of true adoration;
and venerating idols, they
became, in their blind ignorance,
nearly changed into the thing
of stone they had been worshipping.

## Escena IV

Mas no obstante estos delitos,
nunca han faltado centellas
que de aquel primer origen                          530
el noble sér les acuerdan;
y pretendiendo volver
a la dignidad primera,
con lágrimas y suspiros
aplacar a Dios intentan.
Y si no, mirad a Abel,
que las Espigas agrega
y los carbones aplica,
para hacer a Dios ofrenda.

(Ábrese el Carro segundo; y va dando vuelta, en elevación, Abel,
encendiendo la lumbre; y encúbrese, en cantando:)

*Abel*

¡Poderoso Dios                                      540
de piedad inmensa,
esta ofrenda humilde
de mi mano acepta!

*Eco*

Al santo Enoc atended,
que es el primero que empieza
a invocar de Dios el Nombre
con invocaciones nuevas.

(Pasa de la misma manera Enoc, de rodillas, puestas las manos, y
canta:)

*Enoc*

¡Criador Poderoso
del Cielo y la Tierra,

# SCENE 4

[To the cart's playing space come several persons who assume stiff poses and worship the idol. As it is rolled off stage right, a second cart rolls on from stage left.]

*[Echo continues:]*

> But not withstanding all these sins,
> they have not lacked flashes of light,
> sparks to rekindle memories                                    530
> of original nobility;
> and then, attempting to reclaim
> their gift of primal dignity,
> with many tears and heavy sighs,
> they seek to please the Deity.
> And therefore, look on Abel now
> who brings the wheat from harvesting
> and kindles charcoal for the fire
> to give to God an offering.

(The second cart is opened, and on its raised stage is Abel, walking around and lighting the fire; concealing himself, he sings:)

*Abel*

> O Adonai, most powerful,                                      540
> whose mercy knows no boundary,
> deign to take from my poor hand
> this humble offering.

*Echo*

> Attend to holy Enoch, who
> initiated forms of prayer
> which call upon the name of God
> with invocations newly made.

(Enoch crosses the stage in the same way; on his knees and with folded hands, he sings:)

*Enoch*

> O powerful Creator-God
> of lofty heaven and the earth,

sólo a Ti por Dios                                          550
confiesa mi lengua!

*Eco*

Ved a Abraham, aquel monstruo
de la fe y de la obediencia,
que ni dilata matar
al hijo, aunque más lo quiera,
por el mandato de Dios;
ni duda de la promesa
de que al número sus hijos
igualen de las Estrellas.
Y ved cómo Dios benigno,                                   560
en justa correspondencia,
la víctima le perdona
y el sacrificio le acepta.

(Pasa Abraham, como lo pintan, y canta el Ángel:)

*Ángel*

¡Para herir al niño
la mano no extiendas,
que basta haber visto
cuánto al Señor temas!

*Eco*

Ved a Moisés, que Caudillo
de Dios al pueblo gobierna,
y viendo que ha idolatrado                                 570
y Dios castigarlo intenta,
su autoridad interpone
y osadamente Le ruega.

(Pasa Moisés, con las Tablas de la Ley, y canta:)

*Moisés*

¡O perdone al Pueblo,
Señor, Tu clemencia,
o bórreme a mí
de la Vida eterna!

my tongue confesses You alone                    550
as maker of the universe.

### Echo

See Abraham, that prodigy
of faith and of obedience
who did not hesitate to kill
his son, despite his love for him,
because of the command of God,
nor does he doubt that he will see
the number of his progeny
as promised, reach that of the stars.
Now see how God so mercifully,            560
in equal and exact exchange,
gives back his victim-son to him
and yet accepts his sacrifice.

(As described, Abraham crosses the stage [to Isaac], and the angel
sings:)

### Angel

Refrain! Do not extend your hand
to injure your beloved son
when your devout fear of the Lord
is clearly seen by everyone.

### Echo

Behold the leader, called by God,
great Moses, governing his race
who worshiped graven images,            570
and seeing God will punish them,
who boldly pleads before the face
of a just Lord to spare the rod.

(Moses crosses the stage with the tablets of The Law and sings:)

### Moses

O grant pardon to Your people,
according to Your mercy, Lord,
or else, eradicate me
from everlasting life.

*Eco*

Pero ¿para qué es cansaros?
Atended de los Profetas
y Patrïarcas al Coro                                                      580
que con dulces voces tiernas
piden el remedio a Dios,
quieren que a aliviarlos venga.

*Coro 1*

¡Abrid, claros Cielos
vuestras altas puertas,
y las densas nubes
al Justo nos lluevan!

*Eco*

Pues atended, misteriosa,
a otra petición opuesta,
al parecer, a ésta, pues                                                  590
dice con voces diversas:

*Coro 2*

¡Ábranse las bocas
de la dura Tierra,
y brote, cual fruto,
el Salvador de ella!

*Eco*

Con que los unos Le piden
que del Cielo les descienda,
y que de la Tierra nazca
quieren otros, de manera
que ha de tener, Quien los salve,                                         600
entrambas Naturalezas.
Pues yo, ¡ay de mí!, que en Narciso
conozco, por ciertas señas,
que es Hijo de Dios, y que
nació de una verdadera
Mujer, temo, y con bastantes
fundamentos, que Éste sea
el Salvador. Y porque
a la alegoría vuelva
otra vez, digo que temo                                                   610

*Echo*

But why should you exhaust yourselves?
Instead, together, see the prophets
and patriarchs of Israel's nation,                    580
who pray with sweet and tender voices,
petitioning the help of God,
for they desire His salvation.

*First Chorus*

Bright heavens, open wide your gates,
lift up your ancient portals high,
and let the swollen, heavy clouds
rain down the Just One unto us.

*Echo*

Consider, now, the mystery
of the following petition
which speaks in very different words                   590
an apparent contradiction:

*Second Chorus*

Let earth's obdurate, granite womb
travail to open and bring forth
a blossom which becomes the fruit
that saves her from eternal doom.

*Echo*

Now then, some ask that He descend
upon them from the highest heaven,
while others pray that He might bend
His nature to be born from earth,
and thus, earth's savior must combine                 600
both human nature and divine.
Since I, (O miserable me!)
because of certain signs, can see
Narcissus is the Son of God,
born of a woman verily,
sufficient reasons make me fear
that He may be the one who saves.
And thus, returning once again
to allegory, I declare
I greatly fear Narcissus, who                          610

que Narciso, que desdeña
mi nobleza y mi valor,
a aquesta Pastora quiera;
porque suele el gusto,
que leyes no observa,
dejar el brocado
por la tosca jerga.
Y para impedir, ¡ay triste!,
que sobre la injuria hecha
a mi sér y a mi hermosura,                          620
otra mayor no me venga,
hemos de solicitar,
que si impedirle que a verla
no llegue, no sea posible,
que consigamos siquiera
que en las turbias aguas
de su culpa sea,
para que Su imagen
borrada parezca.
¿Qué os parece?

### Soberbia

                    ¿Qué me puede                  630
parecer, si de tu idea
soy, desde que tienes sér,
individua compañera,
tanto, que por asentir
a mis altivas propuestas,
en desgracia de Narciso
estás? Pero aunque desprecia
Él, y toda Su facción,
tus partes y tu nobleza,
ya has visto, que cuando                            640
los demás te dejan,
sólo te acompaña
siempre tu Soberbia.

### Amor Propio

Y yo, que desde el instante
que intentaste tu suprema
Silla sobre el Aquilón
poner, y que tu grandeza
al Altísimo igualara,

disdains all my nobility
and also my equality,
and who may love that shepherdess
because divinely fickle taste
which will not deign to observe laws,
is likely to reject brocade,
preferring rags in which to dress.
And so, in order to prevent
my suffering an injury
against my beauty and myself                    620
much greater yet (O, misery!)
we must negotiate so that
if we cannot wholly repress
His managing to gaze on her,
then we, at least, may find success
by making His reflection dark
in muddy waters that possess
the guilty secret of her sin,
which bars her from her happiness.
What do you think?

### Pride

          What can I think                    630
if your imagination gives
me life? For then you have to be
such an intimate companion,
that, in order to comply
with my arrogant proposals,
you have drawn Narcissus' ire.
But even though He denigrates
you, and with all His faction scorns
your gifts and your nobility,
you have already seen that when                    640
the others leave you faithlessly,
you may be sure your Pride alone
accompanies you eternally.

### Self-Love

And I too, from the instant that
you made it your intent to place
your high throne on the northern wind,
and planned that your magnificence
should equal that of The Most High;

me engendraste, contra ésa
que, representada en visos,                    650
te dieron a entender que era
la que, aunque inferior
en naturaleza,
en mérito había
de ser más excelsa;
y dándote entonces tú
por sentida de la ofensa,
concebiste tal rencor,
engendraste tanta pena,
que en odio mortal,                            660
que en rabiosa queja
se volvió el cariño,
trocó la fineza . . .
Y así, si soy tu Amor Propio,
¿qué dudas que me parezca
bien, que pues padeces tú,
el mundo todo padezca?
¡Padezca esa vil Pastora,
padezca Narciso y muera,
si con muerte de uno y otro                    670
se borran nuestras ofensas!

*Eco*

Pues tan conformes estáis,
y en la elevada eminencia
de esta montaña Se oculta,
acompañado de fieras,
tan olvidado de Sí
que ha que no come cuarenta
días, dejadme llegar
y con una estratagema
conoceré si es Divino,                         680
pues en tanta fortaleza
lo parece, pero luego
en la hambre que Le aqueja
muestra que es Hombre no más,
pues la hambre Le molesta.
Y así yo intento llegar
amorosa y halagüeña,
que la tentación
¿quién duda que sea

you have engendered me against
that one, disguised, about whom you                    650
were made to understand that she,
although by nature's just decree,
was made to be inferior,
would be declared superior,
and in her merit glorified;
and then you, nurturing within
your breast deep feelings of offense,
conceived such animosity
and generated so much pain,
that your affection was transformed          660
to murderous hostility
and all expressions of regard
twisted into mad complaints.
And so, if I am your Self-Love,
can you doubt what seems so clear:
if you must suffer, then it's right
that all the world should suffer too?
Let that vile shepherdess feel pain,
and let Narcissus suffer death,
if by their deaths it comes about          670
that all our sins are blotted out!

### Echo

Since we are in conformity,
and He lives in obscurity,
hiding on a mountain top,
among the rough beasts, wild and rude,
so forgetful of Himself
for forty days, He's had no food,
do give me leave to travel there,
for with a little strategy,
I shall find out if He's divine.            680
Though His endurance seems to be
strong evidence of godliness,
yet hunger tires Him constantly,
and it's the stomach, not the will
that shows a man's humanity.
And thus, I shall appear to Him
flattering and amorous,
for is there anyone who doubts
temptation is more dangerous

más fuerte, si en forma 690
de una mujer tienta?
Y así, vosotros estad,
de todo cuanto suceda,
a la mira.

*Los Dos*

Así lo haremos,
porque acompañarte es fuerza.

---

## Escena V

(Descúbrese un Monte, y en lo alto el Divino Narciso, de Pastor galán, y algunos animales; y mientras Eco va subiendo, dice Narciso en lo alto:)

*Narciso*

En aquesta montaña, que eminente
el Cielo besa con la altiva frente,
sintiendo ajenos, como propios males,
me acompañan los simples animales,
y las canoras aves 700
con músicas süaves
saludan Mi hermosura,
de más luciente Sol, Alba más pura.
No recibo alimento
de material sustento,
porque está desquitando Mi abstinencia
de algún libre bocado la licencia.

(Acaba de subir Eco, y dice cantando en tono recitativo:)

*Eco*

Bellísimo Narciso,
que a estos humanos valles,
del Monte de Tus glorias 710
las celsitudes traes:
mis pesares escucha,

delivered by a woman who                          690
can bring to bear seductive powers?
So you be there, and carefully
observe throughout the hours
what comes to pass.

*Both*

And so we will
because we are inseparable.

---

## SCENE 5

(A mountain appears, and high on the mountain are the Divine
Narcissus, dressed as a young shepherd, and some animals. [Be-
low is Echo, climbing the mountain.] While Echo continues her
way to the top, Narcissus speaks from the summit:)

*Narcissus*

On this mountain, whose high brow
kisses lofty firmament,
the animals, simple and free,
like typical troubles, cling to Me;                700
and the songbirds,
with sweet music,
serenade my comeliness,
like brightest sunlight, purest dawn.
No nourishment do I receive
of any earthly sustenance
because My abstinence forbids
my taking any morsel.

(Echo stops climbing and begins singing in a recitative tone:)

*Echo*

Most beautiful Narcissus,
who brings to human valleys
loftiness and grandeur                              710
from Your glorious mountain,
    give ear to my great sorrow,

indignos de escucharse,
pues ni aun en esto esperan
alivio mis pesares.

Eco soy, la más rica
Pastora de estos valles;
bella decir pudieran
mis infelicidades.

Mas desde que severo                              720
mi beldad despreciaste,
las que canté hermosuras
ya las lloro fealdades.

Pues Tú mejor conoces
que los claros imanes
de Tus ojos arrastran
todas las voluntades,

no extrañarás el ver
que yo venga a buscarte,
pues todo el mundo adora                          730
Tus prendas celestiales.

Y así, vengo a decirte
que ya que no es bastante
a ablandar Tu dureza
mi nobleza y mis partes,

siquiera por Ti mismo
mires interesable
mis riquezas, atento
a tus comodidades.

Pagarte intento, pues                             740
no será disonante
el que venga a ofrecerte
la que viene a rogarte.

Y pues el interés
es en todas edades
quien del Amor aviva
las viras penetrantes,

tiende la vista a cuanto
alcanza a divisarse
desde este monte excelso                          750
que es injuria de Atlante.

Mira aquestos ganados
que, inundando los valles,
de los prados fecundos

and hear my humble story,
though telling it can offer
no easing of my woes.

I am Echo, wealthiest
shepherdess of all these vales;
sadly, grief disqualifies
my claim to be most lovely.

For since You so severely                    720
have scorned my comeliness,
what I once sang as beauty,
I now mourn for as ugly.

Because, better than I,
You know how Your bright eyes
like magnets, irresistibly
attract unwilling hearts,

You will not be surprised
to find me seeking You,
for Your celestial charms                    730
set all the world afire.

And so I come to tell You
that since my pedigree
lacks power to erode
Your adamantine will

perhaps, for your advantage,
you'd look with more attention
upon my wealth, considering
Your needs for bread and wine.

And I, of course, will pay you;              740
between the act of giving
and taking back some profit,
the distance should be narrow.

Mutual self-interest,
remains in every age
the spark that kindles Love's
most penetrating arrows,

so from this lofty mountain,
the burden Atlas bears,
behold the panorama,                         750
with all you can discern.

Gaze on those herds of cattle
filling the whole valley,
and feeding on the emeralds

las esmeraldas pacen.
  Mira en cándidos copos
la leche, que al cuajarse,
afrenta los jazmines
de la Aurora que nace.
  Mira, de espigas rojas,                           760
en los campos formarse
pajizos chamelotes
a las olas del aire.
  Mira de esas montañas
los ricos minerales,
cuya preñez es oro,
rubíes, y diamantes.
  Mira, en el mar soberbio,
en conchas congelarse
el llanto de la Aurora                              770
en perlas orientales.
  Mira de esos jardines
los fecundos frutales,
de especies diferentes
dar frutos admirables.
  Mira con verdes pinos
los montes coronarse:
con árboles que intentan
del Cielo ser Gigantes.
  Escucha la armonía                                780
de las canoras aves
que en coros diferentes
forman dulces discantes.
  Mira de uno a otro Polo
los Reinos dilatarse,
dividiendo regiones
los brazos de los mares,
  y mira cómo surcan
de las veleras naves
las ambiciosas proas                               790
sus cerúleos cristales.
  Mira entre aquellas grutas
diversos animales:
a unos, salir feroces;
a otros, huír cobardes.
  Todo, bello Narciso,

of rich and fertile fields.
　　See milk like alabaster,
that, even in its curdling,
makes pale with shame the jasmine,
Aurora's child, so white.
　　See how, across the fields,　　　　　　760
the ruddy stalks of grain
weave garments which repel
the waves of wind and rain.
　　Behold the mountain range,
gestating mineral wealth,
and bringing forth a treasure
of rubies, diamonds, gold.
　　Look at the proud and swelling sea,
in which the opaque tears of dawn
congeal and mold within their shells　　770
resplendent oriental pearls.
　　Behold those verdant gardens
in which so many kinds
of fertile trees bear fruit
of wondrous quality.
　　See the mountains crown themselves
with coronets of pine,
and overreaching trees aspire
to be the giants of the sky.
　　Listen to the harmony　　　　　　　780
of the songbirds, great and small,
making with their many choirs,
a dulcet woodland symphony.
　　See how realms extend themselves,
from one pole to the other,
and the great sea's azured arms
divide the earth's domains.
　　And see how the ambitious prows
of swiftly-sailing ships slice through
the cerulean crystal waves,　　　　　　790
cutting furrows, like a plow.
　　See there, among those vaulted caves,
the lairs of many animals;
while some emerge ferociously,
the others run off, cowardly.
　　All these, lovely Narcissus,

sujeto a mi dictamen,
son posesiones mías,
son mis bienes dotales.
    Y todo será Tuyo,                                    800
si Tú con pecho afable
depones lo severo
y llegas a adorarme.

*Narciso*

Aborrecida Ninfa,
no tu ambición te engañe,
que Mi Belleza sola
es digna de adorarse.
    Véte de Mi presencia
al polo más distante,
adonde siempre penes,                                    810
adonde nunca acabes.

*Eco*

Ya me voy, pero advierte
que, desde aquí adelante,
con declarados odios
tengo de procurarte
    la muerte, para ver
si mi pena implacable
muere con que Tú mueras,
o acaba con que acabes.

---

## Escena VI

[Paisaje de bosque y prado; y en su extremo, una fuente.]

(Cúbrese el Monte, y sale la Naturaleza Humana)

*Naturaleza Humana*

De buscar a Narciso fatigada,                            820
sin permitir sosiego a mi pie errante,
ni a mi planta cansada
que tantos ha ya días que vagante

are mine to order as I wish,
for they are my possessions,
my portion, and my dowry.
   And all these riches will be Yours,     800
if with a warm and kindly heart,
you put aside severity,
and come, bow down, and worship me.

Abhorred nymph, do not allow
ambition to deceive you,
for only beauty, such as mine,
requires adoration.
   From my presence, now depart,
to the most distant pole,
where you will suffer endlessly     810
and never find surcease or rest.

*Echo*

Already, I am on my way,
but be forewarned that from this day,
with overt hate, I shall seek out
the means to bring about Your death,
   for when You die, then I shall know
if my inexorable pain
will end when You have met Your end
or die as You draw Your last breath.

---

# SCENE 6

[The scene is a forest on one side and a meadow on the other,
with a fountain at the end of the meadow. In the background,]
(the mountain is covered [with clouds]. Human Nature enters.)

*Human Nature*

Fatigued with searching for Narcissus,     820
allowing my rambling feet no rest,
nor pause to tired soles made weary
with many days already spent

examina las breñas
sin poder encontrar más que las señas,
   a este bosque he llegado donde espero
tener noticias de mi Bien perdido;
que si señas confiero,
diciendo está del prado lo florido,
que producir amenidades tantas,                    830
es por haber besado ya Sus plantas.
   ¡Oh, cuántos días ha que he examinado
la selva flor a flor, y planta a planta,
gastando congojado
mi triste corazón en pena tanta,
y mi pie fatigando, vagabundo,
tiempo, que siglos son; selva, que es Mundo!
   Díganlo las edades que han pasado
díganlo las regiones que he corrido,
los suspiros que he dado,                          840
de lágrimas los ríos que he vertido,
los trabajos, los hierros, las prisiones
que he padecido en tantas ocasiones.
   Una vez, por buscarle, me toparon
de la Ciudad las Guardas, y atrevidas,
no sólo me quitaron
el manto, mas me dieron mil heridas
los Centinelas de los altos muros,
teniéndose de mí por mal seguros.
   ¡Oh Ninfas que habitáis este florido           850
y ameno prado, ansiosamente os ruego
que si acaso al Querido
de mi alma encontrareis, de mi fuego
Le noticiéis, diciendo el agonía
con que de amor enferma el alma mía!
   Si queréis que os dé señas de mi Amado,
rubicundo esplendor Le colorea
sobre jazmín nevado;
por su cuello, rizado Ofir pasea;
los ojos, de paloma que enamora                    860
y en los raudales transparentes mora.
   Mirra olorosa de Su aliento exhala;
las manos son al torno, y están llenas
de jacintos, por gala,
o por indicio de Sus graves penas:

examining the rough terrain,
unable to discover more
　　than hints, I've journeyed to this wood,
hoping for news of my lost good.
And, if I rightly read the signs,
the richly flowered meadow boasts
that, to bring forth these buds so sweet,　　　830
it has already kissed His feet.

　　How many days have passed since I
first searched this wood, flower by flower,
plant by plant, while grief devoured
my anguished heart and my tired feet
tread through time, like centuries,
and woods, which span the antipodes.

　　Let the ages that have passed
and the regions I have crossed
bear witness to my endless sighs,　　　840
torrential tears I've shed,
the labors, prisons, and restraints,
I've oft endured with no complaints.

　　Once, the watchmen of the city
accosted me, as I sought Him,
and impudently snatched my mantle,
but worse, the guardsmen of the walls,
sure I was evil, cruelly
gave me a thousand injuries.

　　O nymphs, who live among the blossoms　850
in this meadow, I adjure you,
if you perchance encounter
the best Beloved of my soul,
tell Him the pain of my heart's fire
sickens my soul with love's desire.

　　If you wish, I shall describe my love:
a ruddy splendor tints with color
the snowy jasmine of his skin;
along his neck lie Ophir's curls;
His eyes are like an amorous dove　　　860
that dwells in limpid streams of love.

　　His breath exudes a fragrant myrrh;
His hands extend with upturned palms,
and they are full of hyacinths,
and wounds like bloody, open eyes,

que si el jacinto es Ay, entre Sus brillos
ostenta tantos Ayes como anillos.

Dos columnas de mármol, sobre basas
de oro, sustentan Su edificio bello;
y en delicias no escasas                                  870
suavísimo es, y ebúrneo, el blanco cuello;
y todo apetecido y deseado.
Tal es, ¡oh Ninfas!, mi divino Amado.

Entre millares mil es escogido;
y cual granada luce sazonada
en el prado florido,
entre rústicos árboles plantada,
así, sin que ningún Zagal Le iguale,
entre todos los otros sobresale.

Decidme dónde está El que mi alma adora,   880
o en qué parte apacienta Sus corderos,
o hacia dónde—a la hora
meridiana—descansan sus luceros,
para que yo no empiece a andar vagando
por los rediles, que Lo voy buscando.

Mas, por mi dicha, ya cumplidas veo
de Daniel Sus Semanas misteriosas,
y logra mi deseo
las alegres promesas amorosas
que me ofrece Isaías                                      890
en todas sus Sagradas Profecías.

Pues ya nació aquel Niño hermoso y bello,
y ya nació aquel Hijo delicado,
que será gloria el vello
llevando sobre el hombro el principado:
Admirable, Dios Fuerte, Consejero,
Rey, y Padre del siglo venidero.

Ya brotó aquella Vara misteriosa
de Jesé, la Flor bella en quien descansa
sobre su copa hermosa                                     900
Espíritu Divino, en que afianza
Sabiduría, Consejo, Inteligencia,
Fortaleza, Piedad, Temor y Ciencia.

Ya el Fruto de David tiene la Silla
de Su padre; ya el lobo y el cordero
se junta y agavilla,
y el cabritillo con el pardo fiero;

but as the petals, His hands wear,
like sparkling rings, the wounds he bears.

Marble pillars with gold bases
bear the temple of his body;
white as ivory is His neck,         870
but soft, and lacking no delight;
all for which I yearn and pine,
is, oh nymphs, my Love divine.

From a million, He is chosen;
as a ripened pomegranate
shines amid a flowering meadow,
so is He among wild saplings;
no young shepherd so immense—
none obscures His eminence.

Oh, where is He whom my soul loves?   880
Tell me where He feeds His lambs,
or where, at midday, He gives rest
and sweet repose to His bright eyes.
Let me not wander aimlessly
through the folds where He might be.

But fortunately, I have seen
fulfilled already Daniel's vision
of his mysterious weeks; and with
the happy, loving promises
in all his sacred prophecies,         890
Isaiah sets my heart at ease.

Since there already has been born
that handsome babe and gentle son,
it will be glorious to see
His shoulders bear the primacy:
strong God and Wonder-Counselor,
Eternal Father, mighty King.

Already, Jesse's mystic root
has blossomed forth the beauteous bud
upon whose lovely chalice rests      900
the Holy Spirit, source of wisdom,
counsel, understanding, knowledge,
fear of God, respect, and courage.

Already David's offspring sits
upon His Father's throne; and now
the wolf reclines beside the lamb,
the leopard, with the little goat;

junto al oso el becerro quieto yace,
y como buey el león las pajas pace.

Recién nacido Infante, quieto juega       910
en el cóncavo de áspid ponzoñoso,
y a la caverna llega
del régulo nocivo, Niño hermoso,
y la manilla en ella entra seguro,
sin poderle dañar su aliento impuro.

Ya la señal, que Acaz pedir no quiso,
y Dios le concedió, sin él pedilla,
se ve, pues ya Dios hizo
la nueva, la estupenda maravilla
que a la Naturaleza tanto excede,       920
de que una Virgen pára, y Virgen quede.

Ya a Abraham se ha cumplido la promesa
que Dios reiteró a Isaac, de que serían
en su estirpe y nobleza
bendecidas las gentes que nacían
en todas las naciones,
para participar sus bendiciones.

El Cetro de Judá, que ya ha faltado,
según fue de Jacob la profecía,
da a entender que ha llegado       930
del Mundo la Esperanza y la Alegría,
la Salud del Señor que él esperaba
y en profético espíritu miraba.

Sólo me falta ya, ver consumado
el mayor Sacrificio. ¡Oh, si llegara,
y de mi dulce Amado
mereciera mi amor mirar la cara!
Seguiréle, por más que me fatigue,
pues dice que ha de hallarle quien Le sigue.

¡Oh, mi Divino Amado, quién gozara       940
acercarse a Tu aliento generoso,
de fragancia más rara
que el vino y el ungüento más precioso!
Tu nombre es como el óleo derramado,
y por eso las Ninfas Te han amado.

Tras Tus olores presta voy corriendo:
¡oh, con cuánta razón todas Te adoran!
Mas no estés atendiendo
si del Sol los ardores me coloran;

the calf lies down near the bear's paw,
and, like the ox, the lion eats straw.
  Inside the poisonous asp's den     910
the nursing infant calmly plays;
into the noxious cobra's cave,
in absolute security
the baby puts its arm;
but the snake can do no harm.
  Already the sign made known to him,
without Achaz' requesting it,
is visible, since God has done
a great new thing, a miracle—
a virgin, raised from earth's domain,     920
gives birth, and yet virgin remains.
  Already the promise which was made
to Abraham and then renewed
to his son Isaac is fulfilled,
that all the nations of the earth
partake of blessings and of grace
from his own seed and noble race.
  The reign of Judah now is gone,
in keeping with the prophet's word
to Jacob, that the much desired     930
salvation of the Lord would come,
the hope and joy of all the earth,
this long-awaited, promised birth.
  And now I need only to see
the greater sacrifice fulfilled.
Oh, let it come and privilege me
to see the face of my sweet love!
I'll follow Him, though weariness blinds me;
He says, "who seeks will surely find Me."
  Oh, my divine beloved One,     940
who will enjoy the soft caress
of your sweet breath, fragrance more rare
than choicest wine and precious balm?
Your name is like oil outpoured,
for which, by nymphs You've been adored.
  In haste, do I pursue your fragrance:
oh, with what reason all adore you!
but that the sun's intensity
has darkened me need not dismay you;

mira que, aunque soy negra, soy hermosa, 950
pues parezco a Tu imagen milagrosa.
   Mas allí una Pastora hermosa veo:
¿quién podrá ser beldad tan peregrina?;
mas, o miente el deseo,
o ya he visto otra vez su luz divina.
A ella quiero acercarme,
por ver si puedo bien certificarme.

---

## Escena VII

(Sale la Gracia, de Pastora, cantando; y vanse acercando.)

*Gracia*

Albricias, Mundo; albricias,
Naturaleza Humana,
pues con dar esos pasos 960
te acercas a la Gracia:
¡dichosa el Alma
que merece tenerme en su morada!
   Venturosa es mil veces
quien me ve tan cercana;
que está muy cerca el Sol
cuando parece el Alba:
¡dichosa el Alma
que merece hospedarme en su morada!

(Repite la Música este último verso, y llégase la Naturaleza a ella.)

*Naturaleza Humana*

Pastora hermosa, que admiras, 970
dulce Sirena, que encantas
no menos con tu hermosura
que con tu voz soberana;
pues a mí tu voz diriges
y a mí albricias me demandas
de alguna nueva feliz,
pues dicen tus consonancias:

Behold, though black, yet I am fair,                950
because your countenance I bear.
    But there a shepherdess I see:
who might this wandering beauty be?
Desire deceives me, or perhaps
I've seen her holy light before.
I want to approach her now to see
if worthiness can come to me.

---

## Scene 7

(Enter Grace, dressed as a shepherdess, singing; she and Human
Nature approach each other.)

### Grace

Good tidings, world; good tidings,
oh, happy Human Nature!
for since you set foot on this path,              960
your steps have brought you near to Grace.
Blest is the soul who is worthy
to welcome me into her dwelling!
A thousand times most fortunate
is she who sees me very near;
because we know the Sun is near
the moment that the dawn appears.
Blest is the soul who is worthy
to welcome me into her dwelling!

(The music repeats this last verse, and Human Nature stands
beside her.)

### Human Nature

Wondrous, lovely shepherdess,                     970
sweetest siren who enchants
not at all less with your beauty
than the power of your voice;
since you send your message to me
and ask some show of gratitude,
for the happy news you bring,
in dulcet harmonies:

### Las Dos

Albricias, Mundo; albricias
Naturaleza Humana,
pues con dar esos pasos                    980
te acercas a la Gracia:

### Coro

¡dichosa el Alma,
que merece hospedarme en su morada!

### Naturaleza Humana

¿De qué son? Y tú quién eres
díme; porque aunque tu cara
juzgo que he visto otra vez,
las especies tan borradas
tengo, que no te conozco
bien.

### Gracia

Aquesto no me espanta,
que estuve poco contigo,                   990
y tú entonces descuidada
no me supiste estimar,
hasta que viste mi falta.

### Naturaleza Humana

Pues en fin, díme ¿quién eres?

### Gracia

¿No te acuerdas de una Dama
que, en aquel bello Jardín
adonde fue tu crïanza
por mandato de tu Padre
gustosa te acompañaba
asistiéndote, hasta que                    1000
tú por aquella desgracia,
dejándole a Él enojado,
te saliste desterrada,
y a mí me apartó de ti,
de tu delito en venganza,
hasta ahora?

*The Two*

Good tidings, World; good tidings,
oh, happy Human Nature,
for since you set foot on this path,                980
your steps have brought you near to Grace.

*Chorus*

Blest is the soul who is worthy
to welcome me into her dwelling!

*Human Nature*

What is the Good News? Who are you?
Please tell me, for although I think
that I have seen your face before,
your image is so indistinct
that I can hardly recognize you.

*Grace*

I am not surprised by that
since I was with you so briefly                990
that you, distracted, could not see
how you ought to cherish me
and learned it only by my absence.

*Human Nature*

Then won't you tell me who you are?

*Grace*

Don't you recall a lady who
joyfully accompanied you
in that lovely garden where,
commanded by your Father's will,
you spent your childhood innocence?
I am she who gave you help                1000
till your unfortunate disgrace
had filled His heart with angry fire,
and so, He sent you off in haste,
as punishment for your offense,
and until now, in recompense,
has separated us.

### Naturaleza Humana

¡Oh, venturosa
la que vuelve a ver tu cara,
Gracia divina, pues eres
la mejor prenda del Alma!
¡Los brazos me dá!

### Gracia

Eso no,                                            1010
que todavía te falta
para llegar a mis brazos
una grande circunstancia.

### Naturaleza Humana

Si está en diligencia mía,
díla, para ejecutarla.

### Gracia

No está en tu mano, aunque está
el disponerte a alcanzarla
en tu diligencia; porque
no bastan fuerzas humanas
a merecerla, aunque pueden                         1020
con lágrimas impetrarla,
como dón gracioso que es,
y no es justicia, la Gracia.

### Naturaleza Humana

Y ¿cómo he de disponerme?

### Gracia

¿Cómo? Siguiendo mis plantas,
y llegando a aquella Fuente,
cuyas cristalinas aguas
libres de licor impuro,
siempre limpias, siempre intactas
desde su instante primero,                         1030
siempre han corrido sin mancha,
Aquésta es de los Cantares
aquella Fuente Sellada,
que sale del Paraíso,
y aguas vivíficas mana.

### Human Nature

Oh, blest
is she who sees again your face,
since you remain, Oh Divine Grace,
the human soul's most precious prize!
Open your arms to me!

### Grace

Alas!                                       1010
I cannot by my own volition,
because, to enter my embrace,
you must first meet a great condition.

### Human Nature

If I can, please let me know,
so I can execute this task.

### Grace

You do not hold within your hand
the power to do, but only that
by which you can be open to
receive, for human efforts
cannot deserve it, though one can          1020
with tears, petition that the gift
of Grace be graciously bestowed,
but not as something that is owed.

### Human Nature

And how can I dispose myself?

### Grace

How? By walking in my footsteps
until you come unto that fount
whose waters, clear and crystalline,
free of all impurities,
forever virginal and clean,
which from their entry into time            1030
have always run unsullied;
she is the sealed fountain
of the sacred Song of Songs,
the womb of living waters
flowing out of paradise.

Éste, el pequeño raudal
que, misterioso, soñaba
Mardoqueo, que crecía
tanto, que de su abundancia
se formaba un grande Río,                    1040
y después se transformaba
en Luz y en Sol, inundando
los campos de su pujanza.

### Naturaleza Humana

Ya sé que ahí se entiende Esther
y que, en Esther, figurada
está la imagen divina
de La que es Llena de Gracia.
¡Oh, Fuente divina, oh Pozo
de las vivíficas aguas,
pues desde el primer instante          1050
estuviste preservada
de la original ponzoña,
de la trascendental mancha,
que infesta los demás Ríos:
vuelve tú la imagen clara
de la beldad de Narciso,
que en ti sola se retrata
con perfección Su belleza,
sin borrón Su semejanza!

### Gracia

Naturaleza feliz,                              1060
pues ya te ves tan cercana
a conseguir tu remedio,
llega a la Fuente sagrada
de cristalinas corrientes,
de quien yo he sido la Guarda,
desde que ayer empezó
su corriente, Inmaculada
por singular privilegio;
y encubierta entre estas ramas,
a Narciso esperaremos,                      1070
que no dudo que Lo traiga
a refrigerarse en ella
la ardiente sed que Lo abrasa.

This is the tiny rivulet
of Mordecai's prophetic dream,
in which he saw a little stream
which grew so much that from it did
a great and mighty river rise,                    1040
and that, in turn, transformed itself
into a stream of sun and light,
flooding the fields with its might.

### Human Nature

I understand now that the stream
refers to Esther, and that she
prefigures the divine image
of Mary, who is full of grace.
Oh, fountain divine! oh, well
of living waters! since you
from your first moment of existence,              1050
have been protected and preserved
from the primal, deadly poison,
the transcendental venom which
pollutes all other rivers,
restore the image to clarity
of Narcissus' beauty in me
which is reflected perfectly
in you alone, in whom we see
His likeness in its purity.

### Grace

Oh, Human Nature, fortunate                       1060
since you now see yourself so close
to finding out your remedy,
approach the crystal flowing stream
within the sacred fountain,
whom I have served as guardian
since yesterday, when she began
to rise, immaculately pure
by special dispensation;
now hiding here among these trees,
we shall await Narcissus, whose                   1070
burning thirst sets Him afire
and, doubtless, it will lead Him to
the fountain for a cool libation.

Procura tú que tu rostro
se represente en las aguas,
porque llegando Él a verlas
mire en ti Su semejanza;
porque de ti Se enamore.

### Naturaleza Humana

Déjame antes saludarla,
pues ha de ser ella el medio                    1080
del remedio de mis ansias.

### Gracia

Debido obsequio es, y así
yo te ayudaré a invocarla.

(Canta la Gracia)

¡Oh, siempre cristalina,
clara y hermosa Fuente:
tente, tente;
reparen mi rüina
tus ondas presurosas,
claras, limpias, vivíficas, lustrosas!

### Naturaleza Humana

No vayas tan ligera                             1090
en tu corriente clara;
pára, pára,
mis lágrimas espera:
vayan con tu corriente
santa, pura, clarísima, luciente.

### Gracia

¡Fuente de perfecciones,
de todas la más buena,
llena, llena
de méritos y dones,
a quien nunca ha llegado                        1100
mácula, riesgo, sombra, ni pecado!

### Naturaleza Humana

Serpiente ponzoñosa
no llega a tus espejos:
lejos, lejos

Then try to make your face appear
upon the surface of the waters
so that when He arrives, He might
perceive in you His own reflection,
and give to you all His affection.

### Human Nature

Allow me first to give her greeting
since she must be the remedy                    1080
to heal me of anxiety.

### Grace

What you propose is proper thanks,
so I shall help you call on her.

(Grace sings:)

Oh, fountain ever crystalline,
lucid and lovely,
wait for me, wait for me;
let your clear, life-giving waves,
clear and bright, repair in me
the ruins of my catastrophe.

### Human Nature

Don't go so quickly on your way;                1090
allow your clear current to stay;
delay, delay.
Wait for my tears:
let them dissolve in your pure tide,
clear, full of light, and sanctified.

### Grace

Oh, fountain of perfections
among all the elite:
replete, replete
with virtues and with gifts,
who has never known the pain                    1100
of perilous, dark, or sinful stain.

### Human Nature

The poisonous serpent avoids
your sight persistently:
distantly, distantly

de tu corriente hermosa,
su ponzoña revienta;
tú corres limpia, preservada, exenta.

### Gracia

Bestia obscena, ni fiera,
no llega a tus cristales;
tales, tales                                              1110
son, y de tal manera,
que dan con su dulzura
fortaleza y salud, gusto y ventura.

### Naturaleza Humana

Mi imagen represénta
si Narciso repara,
clara, clara;
porque al mirarla sienta
del amor los efectos,
ansias, deseos, lágrimas y afectos.

### Gracia

Ahora en la margen florida,                               1120
que da a su líquida plata
guarniciones de claveles
sobre campos de esmeraldas,
nos sentaremos en tanto
que llega; que el que Lo atraiga
Naturaleza, no dudo,
si está junta con la Gracia.

### Naturaleza Humana

Si el disponerme a tenerla,
cuanto puedan mis humanas
fuerzas, es lo que me toca,                                1130
ya obedezco lo que mandas.

restricted from your lovely stream,
its poison spreads infectiously,
but you run clean, exempt, and free.

### Grace

No wild or obscene animals
approach your liquid, crystal gate
so great, so great:                                    1110
your crystals are of such a kind
that with their sweetness give a wealth
of pleasure, fortune, strength, and health.

### Human Nature

If Narcissus will behold
my image, there it will appear
so clear, so clear;
and when He sees it, he will feel
the darts of love, its anxious fire,
its tears, affection, and desire.

### Grace

And now, until Narcissus comes,                        1120
let's sit upon the flowery bank
which borders all the silver stream
with garlands of carnations
in fields of shining emeralds;
for the sight of Human Nature
in proximity to Grace
will undoubtedly attract Him.

### Human Nature

If preparing to receive Grace
is the task I have in hand,
then so far as I am able,                               1130
I now obey what you command.

(Llegan las dos a la Fuente; pónese la Naturaleza entre las ramas,
y con ella la Gracia, de manera que parezca que se miran; y sale
por otra parte Narciso, con una honda, como Pastor, y canta el
último verso de (cada una de) las Coplas, y lo demás representa.)

*Narciso*

Ovejuela perdida,
de tu Dueño olvidada,
¿adónde vas errada?
Mira que dividida

(Canta)

de Mí, también te apartas de tu vida.

Por las cisternas viejas
bebiendo turbias aguas,
tu necia sed enjaguas;
y con sordas orejas,                                    1140

(Canta)

de las aguas vivíficas te alejas.

En Mis finezas piensa:
verás que, siempre amante,
te guardo vigilante,
te libro de la ofensa,

(Canta)

y que pongo la vida en tu defensa.

De la escarcha y la nieve
cubierto, voy siguiendo
tus necios pasos, viendo
que ingrata no te mueve                                1150

(Canta)

ver que dejo por ti noventa y nueve.

Mira que Mi hermosura
de todas es amada,

# Scene 8

(The two [enter and] come to the fountain. [Then Human] Nature and Grace position themselves in the thicket in such a way that they appear to be looking at each other; from the other side comes Narcissus, dressed as a shepherd, carrying a sling; he sings the last line of each stanza and acts out the rest.)

*Narcissus*

My little lost lamb,
unmindful of your Master,
where are you wandering?
can you not see

(He sings:)

that you part from life, apart from Me?

Your foolishness
draws you to drink
dirty water from old cisterns,
and your deaf ears compel                                    1140

(He sings:)

you to avoid the life-giving well.

Think about my favors:
you will see, a constant lover,
I watch over you carefully.
I set you free from all offense,

(He sings:)

and I lay down my life in your defense.

Covered with frost and snow,
I continuously follow
in your foolish steps and know
that it moves you not to see                                  1150

(He sings:)

ungrateful one, I leave the ninety-nine for thee.

Behold how much my beauty
is loved by all,

de todas es buscada,
sin reservar criatura,

(Canta)

y sólo a ti te elige tu ventura.

Por sendas horrorosas
tus pasos voy siguiendo,
y Mis plantas hiriendo
de espinas dolorosas                                    1160

(Canta)

que estas selvas producen, escabrosas.

Yo tengo de buscarte;
y aunque tema perdida,
por buscarte, la vida,
no tengo de dejarte,

(Canta)

que antes quiero perderla por hallarte.

¿Así me correspondes,
necia, de juicio errado?
¿No soy Quien te ha crïado?
¿Cómo no me respondes,                                 1170

(Canta)

y (como si pudieras) te Me escondes?

Pregunta a tus mayores
los beneficios Míos:
los abundantes ríos,
los pastos y verdores,

(Canta)

en que te apacentaron Mis amores.

En un campo de abrojos,
en tierra no habitada,
te hallé sola, arriesgada
de lobo a ser despojos,                                1180

(Canta)

y te guardé cual niña de Mis ojos.

is sought by all,
every creature without exception;

(He sings:)

and only you withhold affection.


    In perilous pathways
I follow your footsteps,
constantly wounding My own feet
in craggy woods, where every tree          1160

(He sings:)

grows thorns of piercing cruelty.


    Still, I must search for you:
although I fear that I shall die
if I do not abandon you,
My heart demands that I continue

(He sings:)

and lose My life that I may find you.


    Is it thus that you respond,
foolish one of errant judgment?
Am I not He who nourished thee
Then why do you not answer Me?          1170

(He sings:)

And why (as if you could) do you hide from me?


    Ask your elders, full of years,
about My great beneficence:
about abundant rivers,
the pastures and meadows

(He sings:)

in which My love fed you and gave you repose.


    In a field of thistles
within an empty land,
I found you all alone
with a hungry wolf nearby          1180

(He sings:)

and I guarded you as the apple of My eye.

Trájete a la verdura
del más ameno prado,
donde te ha apacentado
de la miel la dulzura,

(Canta)

y aceite que manó de peña dura.


Del trigo generoso
la medula escogida
te sustentó la vida,
hecho manjar sabroso,                                    1190

(Canta)

y el licor de las uvas oloroso.


Engordaste, y lozana,
soberbia y engreída
de verte tan lucida,
altivamente vana,

(Canta)

Mi belleza olvidaste soberana.


Buscaste otros Pastores
a quien no conocieron
tus padres, ni los vieron
ni honraron tus mayores;                                1200

(Canta)

y con esto incitaste Mis furores.


Y prorrumpí enojado:
Yo esconderé Mi cara
(a cuyas luces pára
su cara el Sol dorado)

(Canta)

de este ingrato, perverso, infiel
    ganado.


Yo haré que Mis furores
los campos les abrasen,
y las hierbas que pacen;
y talen Mis ardores                                     1210

(Canta)

aun los montes que son más superiores.

I carried you to verdant
pastures of delight
where I lay a banquet for you
with sweetness from the honeycomb

(He sings:)

and oil which flows from obdurate stone.

The richest germ, the very heart
of choicest wheat
sustained your life
with bread made savory and fine,                    1190

(He sings:)

and fragrant grapes converted into wine.

You became engorged and slothful,
full of pride and gross conceit;
you saw yourself magnificent,
your pride outshone your sense of duty,

(He sings:)

and you forgot my sovereign beauty.

You went seeking other shepherds
whom your parents did not know,
neither had they ever seen them,
nor did your forbears recognize them               1200

(He sings:)

and you stirred my wrath, for I despise them.

And therefore, did my rage burst forth:
I will turn away My face
without whose light the golden sun
cannot make its face to shine

(He sings:)

on this perverse, ungrateful, faithless flock
of Mine.

I will cause my kindled fury
to devour the fields with flames
and the grass the flock feeds on,
laying waste both with angry heat                  1210

(He sings:)

even the loftiest mountain peak.

Mis saetas ligeras
les tiraré, y la hambre
corte el vital estambre;
y de aves carniceras

(Canta)

serán mordidos, y de bestias fieras.

Probarán los furores
de arrastradas serpientes;
y en muertes diferentes
obrará, en Mis rigores,                    1220

(Canta)

fuera, el cuchillo; y dentro, los
    temores.

Mira que soberano
soy, y que no hay más fuerte;
que Yo doy vida y muerte,
que Yo hiero y Yo sano,

(Canta)

y que nadie se escapa de Mi mano.

Pero la sed ardiente
Me aflige y Me fatiga;
bien es que el curso siga
de aquella clara Fuente,                    1230

(Canta)

y que en ella templar Mi ardor intente.

Que pues por ti he pasado
la hambre de gozarte,
no es mucho que mostrarte
procure Mi cuidado,

(Canta)

que de la sed por ti estoy abrasado.

I will shoot them
with swift arrows,
and famine will cut the stems of life;
on them carnivorous birds will feast,

(He sings:)

and they will be prey of the wild beast.

On them degraded serpents
will test their coiled fury,
and they will feel my awful wrath
in myriad ways of dying:                    1220

(He sings:)

body bleeding from the knife; heart in terror
    crying.

See how powerful I am,
for there is no one stronger;
I put to death, and I give life;
I can wound as well as heal,

(He sings:)

and none can escape my hand's justice and zeal.

But burning thirst
afflicts and tires me;
it is good that to that fountain
I turn my course and there retire          1230

(He sings:)

so that in her I might quench this fire.

For you, I've suffered agony,
an aching hunger to enjoy you,
so it must come as no surprise
that I reveal my great desire:

(He sings:)

thirsting for you, I am on fire.

## Escena IX

[El mismo paisaje, pero con la Fuente en su centro.]

(Todo esto ha de haber dicho llegando hacia la Fuente, y llegando a ella, la mira y dice:)

*Narciso*

> Llego; mas ¿qué es lo que miro?
> ¿Qué soberana Hermosura
> afrenta con su luz pura
> todo el Celestial Zafiro?                    1240
> Del Sol el luciente giro,
> en todo el curso luciente
> que da desde Ocaso a Oriente,
> no esparce en Signos y Estrellas
> tanta luz, tantas centellas
> como da sola esta Fuente.
>     Cielo y Tierra se han cifrado
> a componer su arrebol:
> el Cielo con su Farol,
> y con sus flores el prado.                    1250
> La Esfera se ha transladado
> toda, a quererla adornar;
> pero no, que tan sin par
> Belleza, todo el desvelo
> de la Tierra, ni del Cielo,
> no la pudieran formar.
>
>
>     Recién abierta granada
> sus mejillas sonrosea;
> sus dos labios hermosea
> partida cinta rosada,                         1260
> por quien la voz delicada,
> haciendo al coral agravio,
> despide el aliento sabio
> que así a sus claveles toca;
> leche y miel vierte la boca,
> panales destila el labio.
>     Las perlas que en concha breve

# Scene 9

[The same landscape, but with the fountain at center stage.]
[None of] (the entire speech is spoken while [Narcissus is] approaching the fountain. On His arrival there, and as he gazes at it, [seeing His own reflection.] he says:)

*Narcissus*

> I come; but what is this I see?
> What sovereign beauty puts to flight
> the sapphire of the heavenly sphere,
> which blushes, seeing her pure light?        1240
> The fiery chariot of the sun,
> rolling o'er its shining course
> from occident to orient,
> in signs and stars scatters no force
> of radiance, sparkling and bright
> to match this fountain's light.
> To make the beauty of a sunset,
> the heavens and the earth conspire:
> the field with its scarlet bloom,
> the heavens with their fire.        1250
> Desiring to adorn the fount,
> earth undergoes a transformation;
> but no, all earth's painstaking care
> and all heaven's imagination
> cannot create, nevertheless,
> such unequaled loveliness.

[Narcissus leans over the fountain and gazes into it.]

> It is like a pomegranate,
> blushing to reveal its secret;
> a scarlet ribbon is the mouth,
> parting where its lips have met;        1260
> from behind the teeth like coral,
> comes a voice, soft, sweet, and low,
> on a breath of gentle cadence,
> touching lips with rhythmic flow.
> Honey and milk under the tongue,
> and lips let fall their honeycomb.
> Her pearls contained in a small shell

guarda, se han asimilado
al rebaño, que apiñado
desciende en copos de nieve;　　　　　　　1270
el cuerpo, que gentil mueve,
el aire a la palma toma;
los ojos, por quien asoma
el alma, entre su arrebol
muestran, con luces del Sol,
benignidad de paloma.
　　Terso el bulto delicado,
en lo que a la vista ofrece,
parva de trigo parece,
con azucenas vallado;　　　　　　　　　1280
de marfil es torneado
el cuello, gentil columna.
No puede igualar ninguna
hermosura a su arrebol:
escogida como el Sol
y hermosa como la Luna.
　　Con un ojo solo, bello,
el corazón Me ha abrasado;
el pecho Me ha traspasado
con el rizo de un cabello.　　　　　　　1290
¡Abre el cristalino sello
de ese centro claro y frío,
para que éntre el amor Mío!
Mira que traigo escarchada
la crencha de oro, rizada,
con las perlas del rocío.
　　¡Vén, Esposa, a tu Querido;
rompe esa cortina clara:
muéstrame tu hermosa cara,
suene tu voz a mi oído!　　　　　　　　1300
¡Vén del Líbano escogido,
acaba ya de venir,
y coronaré el Ofir
de tu madeja preciosa
con la Corona olorosa
de Amaná, Hermón y Sanir.

have been likened to a flock,
white and new shorn, gambolling
down the slopes like drifts of snow. 1270
This body's gentle movement has
the palm tree's graceful, dancing air.
As ruby rays shine from the sun
at dusk, so from these eyes so rare,
the soul shines forth with radiant love,
sun-warm and gentle as a dove.

    My eye rejoices in this breast,
so delicately rounded,
like a mound of golden wheat,
with white lilies all around it. 1280
This neck of purest ivory
towers like a graceful column.
None can match the brilliant light
this dawning beauty has become,
unequalled as the sun at noon
and as lovely as the moon.

    A single glance from those bright eyes
has set my heart on fire;
a simple wisp of curly hair
has kindled my desire. 1290
Break the crystalline seal
that guards the clear, cool center,
so that my love may enter!
Now look at how the frost congeals
upon this head of golden curls,
wet with dew like whitest pearls.

    Come, my spouse, to your beloved:
tear away your veil's sheer:
let me see your lovely face;
pour your voice into My ear! 1300
Come from Lebanon, the chosen;
and when you arrive at last,
I shall crown as my Ophir,
the golden treasure of your hair
with the fragrant diadem
of Amana, Hermon and Sanir.

# Escena X

(Quédase como suspenso en la Fuente; y sale eco como acechando.)

*Eco*

¿Qué es aquesto que ven los ojos míos?
O son de mis pesares desvaríos,
o es Narciso el que está en aquella Fuente,
cuya limpia corriente                                          1310
exenta corre de mi rabia fiera.
¡Quién fuera tan dichosa, que pudiera
envenenar sus líquidos cristales
para ponerles fin a tantos males,
pues si Él bebiera en ella mi veneno,
penara con las ansias que yo peno!
Yo me quiero llegar, pues Él, suspenso,
que está templando, pienso,
la sed.

(Llégase, y vuelve a retirarse.)

      ¡Pero qué miro!
Confusa me acobardo y me retiro:                              1320
Su misma semejanza contemplando
está en ella, y mirando
a la Naturaleza Humana en ella.
¡Oh, fatales destinos de mi estrella!
¡Cuánto temí que clara la mirase,
para que de ella no Se enamorase,
y en fin ha sucedido! ¡Oh pena, oh rabia!
Blasfemaré del Cielo que me agravia.
Mas ni aun para la queja
alientos el dolor fiero me deja,                              1330
pues siento en ansia tanta
un áspid, un dogal a la garganta.
Si quiero articular la voz, no puedo
y a media voz me quedo,
o con la rabia fiera
sólo digo la sílaba postrera;
que pues Letras Sagradas, que me infaman,
en alguna ocasión muda me llaman
(porque aunque formalmente

# SCENE 10

([Narcissus] continues leaning over the fountain; Echo enters, as if spying.)

*Echo*

What sight appears before my eyes?
I must be mad with grief, or else
at that clear fount, Narcissus lies;
its limpid waters are still free                          1310
of turbulence from my wild rage.
If only Fate enabled me,
I could poison this clear stream
to end the trouble it has been,
for if He drinks my poison, He
will feel all my anxiety.
Since He is bending over,
quenching His thirst, I think,
I shall approach.

(Echo approaches, but she quickly draws back.)

                        But what do I see?
Confused and daunted, I draw back:                       1320
He is gazing into the fountain,
contemplating His own likeness,
but seeing Human Nature in it.
Oh, fatal Fortune in my stars!
How much I feared He'd see her clearly,
become entranced, and love her dearly,
and at last, it came to pass!
I'll curse the heavens that have wronged me.
But my anger and fierce pain
leave me too breathless to complain,                     1330
and like a rope, my longings clasp
my throat and poison like an asp.
If I wish to speak, I cannot,
left as I am with half a voice
and fiery rage that chokes each word
except the final syllable.
Holy Scriptures, slandering me,
labelled me mute one time before
(though in a strictly formal sense,

serlo no puedo, soylo causalmente                    1340
y eficïentemente, haciendo mudo
a aquel que mi furor ocupar pudo:
locución metafórica, que ha usado
como quien dice que es alegre el prado
porque causa alegría,
o de una fuente, quiere que se ría),
y pues también alguna vez Narciso
enmudecer me hizo,
porque Su Sér Divino publicaba,
y mi voz reprendiéndome atajaba,               1350
no es mucho que también ahora quiera
que, con el ansia fiera,
al llegar a mirarlo quede muda.
Mas ¡ay!, que la garganta ya se anuda;
el dolor me enmudece.
¿Dónde está mi Soberbia? ¿No parece?
¿Cómo mi mal no alienta?
Y mi Amor Propio, ¿cómo no fomenta,
o anima mis razones?
Muda estoy, ¡ay de mí!

---

## Escena XI

(Hace extremos, como que quiere hablar, y no puede; y salen,
como asustados, la Soberbia y el Amor Propio.)

### Amor Propio

                      ¿Qué confusiones     1360
Eco triste lamenta?
Que aunque no es nuevo en ella ver que sienta,
parece nueva pena
la que de sus sentidos la enajena.

### Soberbia

Estatua de sí misma, enmudecida,
ni aun respirar la deja dolorida
la fuerza del ahogo que la oprime,
aunque con mudas señas llora y gime.

I cannot possibly be mute,                                    1340
though causally and efficiently
who sins by anger I make mute:
put metaphorically, it's like
calling the meadow happy
since it causes joy, or a fountain,
funny because it makes one laugh),
and also, at another time,
Narcissus forced me to be mute,
reproaching me, He stopped my voice,
which showed His nature is Divine;                            1350
and thus, it's not surprising He,
observing my anxiety
at seeing Him, silences me.
But ay! Sorrow makes me dumb;
already words stick to my tongue.
Where is my Pride? Won't she appear?
Why does she not relieve my fear?
And my Self-Love, why doesn't he
restore my reasoning to me?
I am dumb! Oh, misery!

---

## SCENE 11

(Echo is agitated as if she wants to speak; Pride and Self-Love
enter fearfully.)

### Self-Love

                        What pain                             1360
does Echo sadly now lament?
Though it's not rare to see her so,
it seems she suffers a new woe,
an alienating sentiment.

### Pride

Her mourning leaves her breathless
and silent as a statue,
weeping and gesturing at you,
so little can her pain express.

### Amor Propio

A consolar lleguemos su lamento,
aunque le sirva de mayor tormento.                    1370

### Soberbia

Lleguemos a saber lo que la enoja,
aunque le sirva de mayor congoja.

### Amor Propio

Pues el tener su Propio Amor consigo,
claro está que será mayor castigo.

### Soberbia

Pues tener su Soberbia, ¿quién ignora
que le será mayor tormento ahora?

### Amor Propio

Mira, que juzgo que precipitada
quiere arrojarse, del furor llevada;
¡tengámosla!

### Soberbia

Tenerla solicito,
aunque yo soy quien más la precipito.                1380

(Lléganse a ella y tiénenla; y ella hace como que quiere arrojarse.)

### Soberbia

¡Tente, Eco hermosa! ¿Dónde vas? Espera;
cuéntanos por qué estás de esa manera,
que despeñarte intentas.
¿Con ver a tu Soberbia no te alientas?
¿Cómo querré yo verte despeñada,
si siempre pretendí verte exaltada?

### Amor Propio

¿Que con ver tu Amor Propio no te animes?
¿Cómo podré sufrir que te lastimes,
si por haberte amado
tanto, nos redujimos a este estado?                  1390

### Self-Love

Though pity may be more tormenting,
let's try to stop her sad lamenting.      1370

### Pride

Let's find out what makes her sad,
though she might feel twice as bad.

### Self-Love

My being with her to lament
is clearly greater punishment.

### Pride

And having Pride, who can deny,
will do naught else but make her cry?

### Self-Love

Look, she's so angry, I can see
that she will jump precipitously.
Let's restrain her.

### Pride

           I shall try,
though I'm the one who's nearly slain her.    1380

(They run to her and take hold of her; she acts as if she wants to throw herself [down a precipice].)

### Pride

Stop, lovely Echo, whither goest?
What drives you to this desperate state?
What brings you to this precipice?
Find solace in my prideful face.
Prime mover of your haughtiness,
I grieve to see you in distress.

### Self-Love

Can it be that the sight of me
can't lift your heart? I'll take no part
in your suicide, for then I and Pride
would have to rue our loving you.      1390

(Todo esto, teniéndola; y desde aquí, va respondiendo.)

*Soberbia*

Tente, pues que yo te tengo.

*Eco*

Tengo.

*Amor Propio*

Refiere tu ansiosa pena.

*Eco*

Pena.

*Soberbia*

Dí la causa de tu rabia.

*Eco*

Rabia.

(Dentro, repite la Música, con tono triste, los ecos.)

*Amor Propio*

Pues eres tan sabia,
¿dínos qué accidentes
tienes, o qué sientes?

*Eco*

Tengo Pena, Rabia . . .                                        1400

*Amor Propio*

¿Pues qué has echado de ver?

*Eco*

De ver.

*Soberbia*

¿De qué estás así, o por qué?

*Eco*

Que.

(They make these speeches while restraining her, and at this
point, she begins to respond.)

*Pride*

Stop it now, because I have you.

*Echo*

I have.

*Self-Love*

Describe for us your anguished pain.

*Echo*

Pain.

*Pride*

Tell us the reason for your rage.

*Echo*

Rage.

(Offstage, Music repeats the echoes in a sad tone.)

*Self-Love*

Now since you are so wise a sage,
can you tell us what transpired,
or what feelings it inspired?

*Echo*

I have pain, rage . . .                              1400

*Self-Love*

Then what have you begun seeing?

*Echo*

Seeing.

*Pride*

What bothers you, and why is that?

*Echo*

That.

*Amor Propio*

¿Hay novedad en Narciso?

*Eco*

Narciso.

*Soberbia*

Dínos, ¿qué te hizo
para ese accidente,
o si es solamente . . .?

*Eco*

De ver Que Narciso . . .                              1410

*Soberbia*

No desesperes aún . . .

*Eco*

Aún.

*Amor Propio*

que aún puede dejar de ser . . .

*Eco*

Ser.

*Soberbia*

que ese barro quebradizo . . .

*Eco*

Quebradizo.

*Amor Propio*

no logre su hechizo,
ni a su Amante obligue.
Mas ¿Él a quién sigue?

*Eco*

A un Sér Quebradizo.                              1420

*Amor Propio*

¿Es posible que la quiere?

*Self-Love*

Is there some news about Narcissus?

*Echo*

Narcissus.

*Pride*

What did he do to you, tell us,
to cause this sudden casualty,
or can it only be . . . ?

*Echo*

From seeing that Narcissus . . .                    1410

*Pride*

Don't give up yet . . .

*Echo*

Yet.

*Self-Love*

that He can yet stop being . . .

*Echo*

Being.

*Pride*

merely clay and very frail . . .

*Echo*

Frail.

*Self-Love*

Your artificial charms may fail
to obligate your lover to you.
But, tell me, whom does He pursue?

*Echo*

A frail being.                                       1420

*Self-Love*

Is she possibly the one He loves?

*Eco*

Quiere.

*Soberbia*

¿Ese agravio me hace a mí?

*Eco*

A mí.

*Amor Propio*

¿Así por ella me agravia?

*Eco*

Me agravia.

*Soberbia*

Pues brote la rabia
de mi furia insana;
pues a una villana . . .

*Eco*

Quiere, A mí Me agravia.                                    1430

*Soberbia*

Juntemos estas voces, que cortadas
pronuncia su dolor despedazadas,
que de ellas podrá ser nos enteremos
por entero, del mal que no sabemos.

*Amor Propio*

Mejor es oírla a ella,
que las repite al són de su querella.

(Dice Eco, con intercadencias furiosas:)

*Eco*

Tengo Pena, Rabia,
De ver Que Narciso
A un Sér Quebradizo
Quiere, A mí Me agravia.                                    1440

(Repite la Música toda la copla.)

*Echo*

He loves.

*Pride*

Does He thus affront me?

*Echo*

Me.

*Self-Love*

Because of her, He thus insults me?

*Echo*

Thus insults me.

*Self-Love*

Then let the tide of my wrath
and rabid rage break out
because a peasant lout . . .

*Echo*

He loves. He thus insults me.                    1430

*Pride*

Let's make sense of isolated
words your sorrow has related,
so from them we can discern
the evil that we've yet to learn.

*Self-Love*

We had better prick our ears
as she laments her fate with tears.

(Echo speaks with frenzied syncopation:)

*Echo*

I have pain and rage
from seeing that Narcissus
loves a frail being
and thus does He insult me.                    1440

(Music repeats the entire stanza.)

*Amor Propio*

En el estéril hueco de este tronco,
la ocultemos, porque el gemido ronco
de sus llorosas quejas
no llegue de Narciso a las orejas;
y allí tristes los dos la acompañemos,
pues apartarnos de ella no podemos.

---

## ESCENA XII

(Vanse, llevándola; y levántase Narciso de la fuente.)

*Narciso*

Selvas, ¿quién habéis mirado,
el tiempo que habéis vivido,
que ame como Yo he querido,
que quiera como Yo he amado?          1450
    ¿A quién, en el duradero
siglo de prolijos días,
habéis visto, selvas Mías,
que muera del mal que muero?
    Mirando lo que apetezco,
estoy sin poder gozarlo;
y en las ansias de lograrlo,
mortales ansias padezco.
    Conozco que ella Me adora
y que paga el amor Mío,          1460
pues se ríe, si Me río,
y cuando Yo lloro, llora.
    No me puedo engañar Yo,
que Mi ciencia bien alcanza
que Mi propia semejanza
es quien Mi pena causó.
    De ella estoy enamorado;
y aunque amor Me ha de matar,
Me es más fácil el dejar
la vida, que no el cuidado.          1470

*Self-Love*

Because the raucous groaning
and her resentful moaning
must not reach Narcissus' ear,
let's hide with her and disappear
into the hollow of a tree,
where we must be with her constantly.

---

## SCENE 12

(They leave, carrying her off, and Narcissus rises from the fountain.)

*Narcissus*

Forests, have you ever known
one who's loved with My desire
or has desired with My fire
in all the years that you have grown?      1450
    In the parade of days gone by,
My forests, whom have you descried
in centuries, who has ever died
of the malady by which I die?
    Gazing, I can only languish:
I can't enjoy her or disdain her;
in my desire to attain her,
I suffer mortal anguish.
    That she adores Me, I can tell,
and repaying love, beguiles,      1460
since if I smile, she also smiles,
and when I weep, she weeps as well.
    I cannot practice self-deception:
my understanding makes it plain
that the cause of all my pain
surely is My own reflection.
    So intensely do I love her,
though love slay Me with its dart,
with My life I'd rather part
than to other loves defer.      1470

(Dice lo siguiente, llegándose hacia donde entró Eco; y ella, desde donde está, va respondiendo.)

*Narciso*

Es insufrible el tormento

*Eco*

Tormento.

*Narciso*

de los dolores que paso

*Eco*

Paso.

*Narciso*

en rigor tan insufrible;

*Eco*

Insufrible.

*Narciso*

pues en mi pena terrible
y en el dolor de que muero,
no gozando lo que quiero,

*Los Dos*

Tormento Paso Insufrible.                           1480

*Narciso*

¡Oh cómo estará después

*Eco*

Pues.

*Narciso*

maltratada Mi Hermosura,

*Eco*

Mi Hermosura.

(He speaks the following when he arrives at the place where Echo enters and she responds from where she is.)

*Narcissus*

How agonizing is the pain

*Echo*

Pain.

*Narcissus*

of the sorrows that I suffer

*Echo*

I suffer.

*Narcissus*

in torture so unbearable

*Echo*

Unbearable.

*Narcissus*

since in My pain, so terrible
and grief from which I must expire,
deprived of all My heart's desire,

*The Two*

I suffer unbearable pain.                    1480

*Narcissus*

Oh, what will the result be, then

*Echo*

Then.

*Narcissus*

for My disfigured beauty

*Echo*

Beauty.

*Narciso*

de todas la más cabal!

*Eco*

Cabal.

*Narciso*

Pues Mi pena sin igual
me sujetó a padecer;
pues ha ultrajado Mi Sér.

*Los Dos*

Pues Mi hermosura Cabal . . .                    1490

*Narciso*

¡Que haya podido el Amor

*Eco*

El Amor.

*Narciso*

sujetar así a Narciso,

*Eco*

Hizo.

*Narciso*

y arrastrar a lo Inmortal!

*Eco*

Mortal.

*Narciso*

Por él padezco este mal
que siente mi pena fiera,
pues a Aquél que Inmortal era,

*Los Dos*

El amor Hizo Mortal.                             1500

*Narciso*

¿Cómo tan fiera sujeta

*Narcissus*

of all beauties, unsurpassed?

*Echo*

Unsurpassed.

*Narcissus*

Since My unequalled agony
subjected Me to suffering,
it has abused My very being,

*The Two*

Then My beauty, unsurpassed . . .                    1490

*Narcissus*

To think it possible that love

*Echo*

Love.

*Narcissus*

subdued Narcissus, and thus made

*Echo*

Made.

*Narcissus*

merely finite the immortal!

*Echo*

Mortal.

*Narcissus*

By My suffering this evil,
which causes Me great agony,
the One with immortality

*The Two*

love made mortal.                                    1500

*Narcissus*

Why am I so cruelly subject

*Eco*

Sujeta.

*Narciso*

aquesta pena inhumana

*Eco*

Humana.

*Narciso*

Mi Ser Divino impasible?

*Eco*

Pasible.

*Narciso*

Mas sin duda es invencible
del Amor la fortaleza,
pues ha puesto a Mi Belleza

*Los Dos*

Sujeta, Humana, Pasible.                                    1510

*Música y Él*

Tormento Paso Insufrible;
Pues Mi Hermosura Cabal
El Amor Hizo Mortal,
Sujeta, Humana, Pasible.

*Narciso*

Osadamente el Amor

*Eco*

El Amor.

*Narciso*

quiso mostrar lo que puede

*Eco*

Que puede.

*Narciso*

con sus saetas herir;                                        1520

*Echo*

Subject.

*Narcissus*

to that torture, so inhuman

*Echo*

Human.

*Narcissus*

though divine, invulnerable?

*Echo*

Vulnerable.

*Narcissus*

But without doubt, invincible
is love in its great potency
since it has made My loveliness

*The Two*

Subject, Human, Vulnerable.                    1510

*Music and He*

I suffer pain unbearable
since love imposed mortality
upon My beauty unsurpassed,
subject, human, vulnerable.

*Narcissus*

Audaciously did love

*Echo*

Love.

*Narcissus*

wish to demonstrate it can

*Echo*

Can.

*Narcissus*

with its arrows deeply wound.

*Eco*

Herir.

*Narciso*

pues ¿quién Me pudo inducir
a que tan penoso viva,
sino, con su fuerza activa,

*Los Dos*

El Amor, Que puede Herir?

*Narciso*

Y poniendo el blanco en Mí,

*Eco*

En mí.

*Narciso*

todo su poder mostró,

*Eco*

Mostró.

*Narciso*

ostentando su pujanza;

*Eco*

Su pujanza.                                                    1530

*Narciso*

pues bajando la balanza
de Mi Deidad soberana
por igualarla a la humana,

*Los Dos*

En mí Mostró Su pujanza.

*Narciso*

Triste está Mi alma, y amando,

*Eco*

Y amando.

Wound. 1520

*Narcissus*

Then how could I be importuned
to live My life so painfully
except by force, used brutally?

*The Two*

Love, which can so deeply wound,

*Narcissus*

has placed its target deep in Me,

*Echo*

In me.

*Narcissus*

and all its power has shown forth,

*Echo*

Has shown forth.

*Narcissus*

exhibiting its potency,

*Echo*

Its potency. 1530

*Narcissus*

thus creating parity
between My sovereign Deity
and My acquired humanity.

*The Two*

In Me, love's shown its potency.

*Narcissus*

My soul is sad and loving,

*Echo*

And loving.

*Narciso*

y sin atender a Mí,

*Eco*

A mí.

*Narciso*

por buscar Mi semejanza.

*Eco*

Semejanza.                                                                                          1540

*Narciso*

¿Quién el misterio no alcanza
de los suspiros que doy?
Que admira el ver cuál estoy,

*Los Dos*

Y amando A mi Semejanza.

*Narciso*

De Mi Solio, que es del Cielo,

*Eco*

Del Cielo.

*Narciso*

manso y amoroso vine,

*Eco*

Vine.

*Narciso*

sin ver que bajé a morir.

*Eco*

A morir.                                                                                            1550

*Narciso*

Ninguno podrá medir
lo grande de Mi fineza;
pues sin mirar Mi Grandeza,

*Narcissus*

and without harkening to My . . .

*Echo*

My.

*Narcissus*

need to find My own reflection,

*Echo*

Reflection                                        1540

*Narcissus*

or hearing My sighs of rejection,
who can resolve My mystery
and learn of My identity?

*The Two*

And loving My reflection.

*Narcissus*

From My throne, which is in heaven,

*Echo*

In heaven.

*Narcissus*

meek and amorous, I came,

*Echo*

Came.

*Narcissus*

not seeing that I came to die.

*Echo*

To die.                                            1550

*Narcissus*

No one can ever quantify
My gift's great worth, with certitude,
unless she sees My magnitude.

*Los Dos*

Del Cielo Vine A morir.

*Música y Él*

El Amor, Que puede Herir,
En Mí Mostró Su pujanza;
Y amando A Mi semejanza,
Del Cielo Vine A morir.

*Narciso*

Mas ¿quién, en el tronco hueco,

*Eco*

Eco.                                          1560

*Narciso*

con triste voz y quejosa,

*Eco*

Quejosa.

*Narciso*

así a mis voces responde?

*Eco*

Responde.

*Narciso*

¿Quién eres, oh voz; o dónde
te ocultas, de Mí escondida?
¿Quién Me responde afligida?

*Los Dos*

Eco Quejosa Responde.

*Narciso*

Pues ya, con lo que estás viendo,

*Eco*

Viendo.                                       1570

*The Two*

I came from heaven to die.

*Music and He*

Love, which can so deeply wound,
in Me has shown its potency;
and therefore, loving My reflection,
I came from heaven to die.

*Narcissus*

With sorrowful voice, complaining,

*Echo*

Complaining. 1560

*Narcissus*

and grief, not held in check; oh,

*Echo*

Echo.

*Narcissus*

To my outcry she thus responds?

*Echo*

Thus responds.

*Narcissus*

Who is within the tree trunk's hollow?
Oh, voice, where do you hide from me?
And who cries out so piteously?

*The Two*

Complaining Echo thus responds.

*Narcissus*

Through what perspective are you seeing?

*Echo*

Seeing. 1570

*Narciso*

¿tu despecho qué hay que quiera,

*Eco*

Que quiera.

*Narciso*

ni que espere más tu amor?

*Eco*

Tu amor.

*Narciso*

Pues sin conocer tu error,
de tu Amor Propio guïada,
andas solamente errada,

*Los Dos*

Viendo Que quiera Tu amor.

*Narciso*

¡Si ves que siempre he de amar

*Eco*

Amar.                                                    1580

*Narciso*

y que he de estar en un sér;

*Eco*

Un sér.

*Narciso*

que aunque juzgas inferior

*Eco*

Inferior.

*Narciso*

el objeto de Mi amor
que tu soberbia desdeña

despair of having what you want?

You want.

or that which hopes for more—your love?

Your love.

But since you have no concept of
your error, guided by your own
Self-Love, you wander all alone,

*The Two*

Seeing that you want your love.

If you see I always have to love

To love.                                                        1580

and to live within a being,

A being.

though you judge her so inferior,

So inferior.

My wisdom shows Me that superior
to all others is My bride,

Mi propia Bondad me enseña

*Los Dos*

Amar a Un sér Inferior!

*Narciso*

Yo tengo de amar; y así,

*Eco*

Y así.                                               1590

*Narciso*

no esperes verme a tus ojos,

*Eco*

A tus ojos.

*Narciso*

de quien Mi Beldad se esconde.

*Eco*

Se esconde.

*Narciso*

Porque nunca corresponde
tu soberbia a la humildad
que apetece Mi Beldad;

*Los Dos*

Y así, A tus ojos Se esconde.

*Eco y Música*

Eco Quejosa Responde,
Viendo Que quiera Tu amor                            1600
Amar un sér Inferior;
Y así, A tus ojos Se esconde.

(Va llegando Narciso a la Fuente, y dice:)

*Narciso*

Mas ya el dolor Me vence. Ya, ya llego
al término fatal por Mi querida:

whom you disdain in foolish pride,

*The Two*

To love a being so inferior.

*Narcissus*

I must forever love, and so,

*Echo*

And so.                                                    1590

*Narcissus*

don't hope to see Me; from your eyes,

*Echo*

From your eyes.

*Narcissus*

all My beauty is concealed.

*Echo*

Is concealed.

*Narcissus*

Since never has your pride revealed
the measure of humility
that My beauty asks of thee,

*The Two*

so, from your eyes it is concealed.

*Echo and Music*

Complaining Echo answers,
seeing that you want your love                    1600
to love a being so inferior,
she is concealed from your eyes.

(Narcissus approaches the fountain and says:)

*Narcissus*

Now my sorrow conquers Me. I aspire
at last, to meet my death, to give love all;

que es poca la materia de una vida
para la forma de tan grande fuego.

    Ya licencia a la Muerte doy: ya entrego
el Alma, a que del Cuerpo la divida,
aunque en ella y en él quedará asida
Mi Deidad, que las vuelva a reunir luego.     1610

    Sed tengo: que el amor que Me ha abrasado,
aun con todo el dolor que padeciendo
estoy, Mi Corazón aún no ha saciado.

    ¡Padre! ¿Por qué en un trance tan tremendo
Me desamparas? Ya está consumado.
¡En Tus manos Mi Espíritu encomiendo!

---

## Escena XIII

(Suena terremoto; cae Narciso dentro del vestuario; y salen asustados Eco, la Soberbia y el Amor Propio.)

*Eco*

¡Qué eclipse!

*Soberbia*

    ¡Qué terremoto!

*Amor Propio*

¡Qué asombro!

*Eco*

    ¡Qué horror!

*Soberbia*

        ¡Qué susto!

*Eco*

¡Las luces del Sol apaga
en la mitad de su curso!     1620

*Amor Propio*

¡Cubre de sombras el Aire!

and yet, the matter of my life seems small
for kindling and sustaining such a fire.
     Though I have licensed Death to capture Me,
to separate my soul and fleshly part,
from neither will divinity depart,
and they will be rejoined eternally.          1610
     I thirst: for love that has been burning Me,
has not my heart's desire diminished,
despite the pain I bear I do not fear it.
     My Father, why do You abandon Me
to this dark swoon of death? It is finished.
Into your hands, I give my spirit!

---

## Scene 13

(An earthquake is heard; Narcissus falls [and dies] behind the
side curtains; enter Echo, Pride, and Self-Love, frightened.)

*Echo*

What an eclipse!

*Pride*

What an earthquake!

*Self-Love*

What a shock!

*Echo*

What horror!

*Pride*

What fright!

*Echo*

The wheels of the sun's chariot
stop moving in mid-course!          1620

*Self-Love*

The air is heavy with shadows!

*Soberbia*

¡Viste a la Luna de luto!

*Eco*

La Tierra, de su firmeza
desmintiendo el atributo,
pavorosa se estremece,
y abriendo su centro oculto,
escondiendo en él los montes,
manifiesta los sepulcros.

*Soberbia*

Las piedras, enternecidas,
rompiendo su ceño duro                                    1630
se despedazan, mostrando
que aun en lo insensible cupo
el sentimiento.

*Eco*

                       Y lo más
portentoso que descubro,
es que no causa este eclipse
aquel natural concurso
del Sol y la Luna, cuando
—los dos luminares juntos
en perpendicular línea—
la interposición del uno                                  1640
no nos deja ver al otro,
y así el Sol parece obscuro,
no porque él lo esté, sinó
porque no se ven sus puros
resplandores. Pero ahora,
siguiendo apartados rumbos,
distantes están, y así
ningún Astro se interpuso
a ser de su luz cortina,
sino que él, funesto y mustio,                            1650
sus resplandores apaga,
como si fueran caducos.

### Pride

The moon dresses herself in remorse!

### Echo

Controverting ancient theory
that she has great stability,
the earth is trembling fearfully;
and opening her secret womb
that hides its embryonic mountains,
she shows within it hidden tombs.

### Pride

The rocks are moved to rare compassion,
which cracks their adamantine faces;      1630
they split asunder, showing that
sorrowing can leave its traces
even in the obdurate.

### Echo

         And most
portentous is the fact
that the eclipse has not been caused
by the natural, exact
convergence of the sun and moon—
for when the two are in a line
perpendicular to earth,
the intervention of the one      1640
blocks our vision of the sun,
and thus, the sun appears obscured,
not because it really is,
but because, in its full splendor,
it cannot be observed. But now,
in separate paths they make their rounds,
and they are distant from each other;
and thus no star has intervened
to intercept the sun's bright light,
but he himself, mournful and sick,      1650
snuffs out all his resplendent flames
like a worn-out taper's wick.

Y quizá por haber eso
observado, en el tumulto
donde todo el Universo
sirve de pequeño vulgo,
algún Astrólogo grande
prorrumpe en la voz que escucho
entre la asombrada turba,
pues dice en ecos confusos:                    1660

(Dentro)

¡O padece el Autor del Universo,
o perece la máquina del Mundo!

*Amor Propio*

¡Oh fuerza de Amor! ¡Oh fuerza
de un enamorado impulso:
pasar la línea a la Muerte,
romper al Infierno el muro,
porque el haberse rendido
Le sirva de mayor triunfo!
Mas atended, que en la turba                    1670
otra voz distinta escucho:

(Dentro)

¡Este Hombre, de verdad era muy Justo!

*Soberbia*

Otra voz no menos clara,
o la misma, con orgullo
de la Fe, y admiración,
confiesa con otros muchos:

(Dentro)

¡Éste era Hijo de Dios, yo no lo dudo!

*Eco*

¡Oh, pese a mí, que ya empieza
Su Muerte a mostrar el fruto
de aquel misterioso Grano
que escondido en el profundo                    1680

*Self-Love*

And perhaps since he has seen
in the chaos and melee
that the universe now seems
a single small community,
some eminent astrologer
breaks forth into these words I hear
as confusing echoing
in a crowd gone wild with fear:　　　　　　1660

(From within)

The author of the universe is suffering,
or else the world machine is perishing!

*Self-Love*

Oh sovereign is the strength of love
and that lover unrestrained
who strides across the line to death
and breaks apart the wall of hell,
for in surrendering Himself
in greater triumph He will dwell!
But wait, since from the crowd I hear
another voice both loud and clear:　　　　　1670

(From within)

Without a doubt, this man was just!

*Pride*

And one with no less clarity,
perhaps the same, with faith-filled pride
and admiration does confess
with many others to profess:

(From within)

In truth, this was the Son of God!

*Echo*

Oh, woe is me! So soon His death
begins to manifest the fruit
of that mysterious seed which lay
well hidden in the depths of earth　　　　　1680

pareció muerto, y después
tantas espigas produjo!
¡Oh, nunca la profecía
se oyera, en labios impuros,
de que para vivir todos
fue menester morir Uno!
¡Oh, nunca, engañada y ciega,
solicitara por rumbos
tan diferentes Su Muerte,
pues cuando vengada juzgo                    1690
mi afrenta con que Él muriese,
hallo que todo mi estudio
sirvió de ponerle medios
para que Su amante orgullo
la mayor fineza obrase,
muriendo por Su trasunto!
Mas aunque la envidia fiera
despedaza, áspid sañudo,
mi pecho, ya por lo menos
tengo el consuelo (si pudo                    1700
caber en mí algún consuelo)
de conseguir que en el Mundo
no esté a los ojos de aquella
Villana; que de su rudo
natural, y de su ingrata
condición, no será mucho
que, no viéndolo, Lo olvide.

*Amor Propio*

Dices muy bien; que no dudo
que, no viéndolo a sus ojos,
olvidada de los sumos                         1710
beneficios que Le debe,
volverá a seguir el curso
de sus delitos pasados:
que acostumbrados insultos
con dificultad se olvidan,
no habiendo quien del discurso
los esté siempre borrando
con encontrados asuntos
de diferentes recuerdos.

and seeming dead, has then produced
so many ears of golden grain!
If only the prophetic word
from impure lips had not been heard,
declaring that for all to live
it was required that one must die!
Oh, that you, deceived and blind,
had n'er gone forth to seek and find
His death along such various paths,
since when I weigh my vengeful wrath                    1690
against the power of His oblation,
I find that all my machinations
served to place the means before Him
so that His loving haughtiness
could thus achieve the great finesse,
that, for His image, He gave His life!
But even though fierce jealousy,
which poisons like a furious asp,
within my breast may cause great strife,
at least there is some consolation                    1700
(if consolation touches me.)
I know on earth He will not see
Himself reflected in the eyes
of that crude peasant; who when she
no longer sees Him, will forget Him
since Her nature is so rude,
full of crass ingratitude.

### Self-Love

You make good sense; and I suppose
that when she can with her own eyes
no longer see Him, she'll forget                    1710
the lofty benefits she owes,
and she will follow once again
the path of her past sins and woes:
the deeply ingrained course of sin
that is not easy to efface
when there is no one constantly
from her thinking to erase
sinful thoughts and to replace
them all with different memories.

### Soberbia

Pues sea ahora nuestro estudio                    1720
solicitar que ella olvide
estos beneficios Suyos;
porque si después de tantos
Le vuelve a ofender, no dudo
que a ella ocasione más pena,
y a nosotros mayor triunfo.

### Eco

Bien decís. Mas ella viene
llorando como infortunio
la que es su dicha mayor,
con el piadoso concurso                           1730
de las Ninfas y Pastores.
Esperemos aquí ocultos,
hasta ver en lo que paran
tantos funestos anuncios.

### Pride

Then, let it be our present plan          1720
to see that she quite thoroughly
forgets those benefits of His;
for she, who has received so many,
need only once more to offend,
and I don't doubt that she will suffer,
and we shall triumph in the end.

### Echo

That's well said, but here she comes
with a pious company
of nymphs and shepherds, and she weeps
like misery itself, for tears          1730
her greatest happiness must be.
Let's wait here and hide ourselves
until we witness the conclusion
of dismal omens in profusion.

# Escena XIV

(Retíranse a un lado; y sale la Naturaleza llorando, y todas las Ninfas, y Pastores, y Música triste.)

### Naturaleza Humana

Ninfas habitadoras
de estos campos silvestres,
unas en claras ondas
y otras en troncos verdes;
    Pastores, que vagando
estos prados alegres,                    1740
guardáis con el ganado
rústicas sencilleces:
    de mi bello Narciso,
gloria de vuestro albergue,
las dos divinas lumbres
cerró temprana muerte:
    ¡sentid, sentid mis ansias;
llorad, llorad Su Muerte!

### Música

¡Llorad, llorad Su muerte!

### Naturaleza Humana

Muerte Le dio Su amor;                   1750
que de ninguna suerte
pudiera, sino sólo
Su propio amor vencerle.
    De mirar Su retrato,
enamorado muere;
que aun copiada Su imagen,
hace efecto tan fuerte:
    ¡sentid, sentid mis ansias:
llorad, llorad Su Muerte!

### Música

¡Llorad, llorad Su Muerte!               1760

# Scene 14

([Echo, Pride, and Self-Love] retire to one side; enter Human Nature, weeping, and [with her] all the nymphs and shepherds as well as sad Music. )

### Human Nature

You nymphs, inhabitants
of wild fields and seas,
some in the crystal waves,
others in trunks of trees;
   Shepherds, you who wander
in meadows happily                                    1740
keeping watch over your flocks
with natural simplicity:
   untimely death extinguished
the two divine lights of the face
of my beautiful Narcissus,
glory of your dwelling place:
   feel, oh feel my anguish;
mourn, oh mourn His death!

### Music

Mourn, oh mourn His death!

### Human Nature

His love gave Him to Death.                           1750
Not Fortune's power or deceit,
but only His own love
could lead Him to defeat.
   Seeing His own portrait
in her, copied and disguised,
so great in its effect:
He loves it, and He dies.
   Feel, oh feel my anguish;
mourn, oh mourn His death!

### Music

Mourn, oh mourn His death!                            1760

*Naturaleza Humana*

Ver su malogro, todo
el Universo siente:
las peñas se quebrantan,
los montes se enternecen;
   enlútase la Luna,
los Polos se estremecen,
el Sol su luz esconde,
el Cielo se obscurece.
   ¡Sentid, sentid mis ansias;
llorad, llorad Su Muerte!                    1770

*Música*

¡Llorad, llorad Su Muerte!

*Naturaleza Humana*

El Aire se encapota,
la Tierra se conmueve,
el Fuego se alborota,
el Agua se revuelve.
   Abren opacas bocas
los sepulcros patentes,
para dar a entender
que hasta los muertos sienten.
   ¡Sentid, sentid mis ansias;                1780
llorad, llorad Su Muerte!

*Música*

¡Llorad, llorad Su Muerte!

*Naturaleza Humana*

Divídese del Templo
el velo reverente,
dando a entender que ya
se rompieron sus Leyes.
   El Universo todo,
de Su Beldad doliente,
capuz funesto arrastra,
negras bayetas tiende.                         1790
   ¡Sentid, sentid mis ansias;
llorad, llorad Su Muerte!

*Human Nature*

The entire universe
mourns His sad, untimely end
with mountains moved to pity
and rocks that split and rend;
    the moon dresses in mourning,
the sun conceals its light,
the poles tremble and shake,
and heaven grows dark with fright.
    Feel, oh feel my anguish;
mourn, oh mourn His death!         1770

*Music*

Mourn, oh mourn His death!

*Human Nature*

The air is overcast,
earth is agitated,
fire leaps out of control,
waters boil unabated.
    The sealed sepulchers
open their dark mouths wide
demonstrating clearly
that even the dead have cried.
    Feel, oh feel my anguish;        1780
mourn, oh mourn His death!

*Music*

   Mourn, oh mourn His death!

*Human Nature*

The veil of the temple
is torn from top to floor
making it known that now
its laws are intact no more.
    The entire universe,
mourning His loveliness,
drags its sad and ancient cloak,
spreads black baize in its distress.     1790
    Feel, oh feel my anguish;
mourn, oh mourn His death.

*Música*

¡Llorad, llorad Su Muerte!

*Naturaleza Humana*

¡Oh vosotros, los que
vais  pasando, atendedme,
y mirad si hay dolor
que a mi dolor semeje!
    Sola y desamparada
estoy, sin que se llegue
a mí más que el dolor,                          1800
que me acompaña siempre.
    ¡Sentid, sentid mis ansias;
llorad, llorad Su Muerte!

*Música*

¡Llorad, llorad Su Muerte!

*Naturaleza Humana*

De la fuerza del llanto
mi rostro se entumece,
y se ciegan mis ojos
con lágrimas que vierten.
    Mi corazón, en medio
de mi pecho, parece                             1810
cera que se derrite
junto a la llama ardiente.
    ¡Sentid, sentid mis ansias;
llorad, llorad Su Muerte!

*Música*

¡Llorad, llorad Su Muerte!

*Naturaleza Humana*

Mirad Su Amor, que pasa
el término a la Muerte,
y por mirar Su imagen
al Abismo desciende;
    pues sólo por mirarla,                      1820
en las ondas del Lethe
quebranta los candados
de diamantes rebeldes.

*Music*

Mourn, oh mourn His death.

*Human Nature*

Oh you, who are going
on your way, hear me,
and see if any sorrow
exceeds my agony.
   I am alone and helpless,
for no one comes to me
with any aid, and sorrow                    1800
is all my company.
   Feel, oh feel my anguish;
mourn, oh mourn His death!

*Music*

Mourn, oh mourn His death!

*Human Nature*

My face is much inflamed
with floods of teary brine
and with the stormy weeping,
my eyes are nearly blind.
   Deep within my breast
my sad heart shrinks the same               1810
as solid wax that melts
next to the burning flame.
   Feel, oh feel my anguish;
mourn, oh mourn His death!

*Music*

Mourn, oh mourn His death!

*Human Nature*

See His Love, which dares
Death's limits to dismiss,
and, seeking for His image,
descends to the abyss;
   for only seeing it                        1820
submerged in Lethe's spell
can He break the diamond,
resistant locks of hell.

¡Sentid, sentid mis ansias;
llorad, llorad Su Muerte!

*Música*

¡Llorad, llorad Su Muerte!

*Naturaleza Humana*

¡Ay de mí, que por mí
Su Hermosura padece!
Corran mis tristes ojos
de lágrimas dos fuentes.                    1830
  Buscad Su Cuerpo hermoso,
porque con los ungüentes
de preciosos aromas
ungirlo mi amor quiere.
  ¡Sentid, sentid mis ansias;
llorad, llorad Su Muerte!

*Música*

¡Llorad, llorad Su Muerte!

*Naturaleza Humana*

Buscad mi Vida en esa
imagen de la muerte,
pues el darme la vida                       1840
es el fin con que muere.

(Hacen que Lo buscan.)

Mas, ¡ay de mí, infeliz,
que el Cuerpo no parece!
Sin duda Le han hurtado:
¡Oh, quién pudiera verle!

(Sale la Gracia.)

*Gracia*

Ninfa bella, ¿por qué
lloras tan tiernamente?
¿Qué en este sitio buscas?
¿Qué pena es la que sientes?

Feel, oh feel my anguish;
mourn, oh mourn His death!

*Music*

Mourn, oh mourn His death!

*Human Nature*

Woe is me, that for me
His beauty should languish!
May my sad eyes ever be
two fountains full of anguish.                    1830
    Seek for His lovely body
because my heart's contentment
depends upon anointing it
with rare and perfumed ointment.
    Feel, oh feel my anguish;
mourn, oh mourn His death!

*Music*

Mourn, oh mourn His death!

*Human Nature*

Seek my life in that bright
image of His death
since He sacrificed His life                       1840
to give me vital breath.

(They go about as if seeking Him.)

But I am painfully bereft,
for His body is not there!
Surely they have stolen Him:
Who has seen Him anywhere?

(Enter Grace.)


*Grace*

Oh, lovely nymph, why do you
lament so piteously?
What are you seeking in this place?
Reveal your agony.

### Naturaleza Humana

Busco a mi Dueño amado; 1850
ignoro dónde ausente
Lo ocultan de mis ojos
los hados inclementes.

### Gracia

¡Vivo está tu Narciso;
no llores, no lamentes,
ni entre los muertos busques
Al que está Vivo siempre!

---

## ESCENA XV

(Sale Narciso, con otras galas, como Resucitado, por detrás de la
Naturaleza; y ella se vuelve a mirarlo.)

### Narciso

¿Por qué lloras, Pastora?
Que las perlas que viertes
el Corazón Me ablandan, 1860
el Alma Me enternecen.

### Naturaleza Humana

Por mi Narciso lloro,
Señor; si Tú Le tienes,
díme dónde está, para
que yo vaya a traerle.

### Narciso

¿Pues cómo, Esposa Mía,
no puedes conocerme,
si a Mi Beldad Divina
ninguna se parece?

### Naturaleza Humana

¡Ay, adorado Esposo, 1870
deja que alegremente
llegue a besar Tus plantas!

*Human Nature*

I seek my cherished Lord;                   1850
I know not where He lies,
because untimely destiny
conceals Him from my eyes.

*Grace*

Your Narcissus lives;
weep not so piteously,
nor look among the dead.
He lives eternally.

---

## SCENE 15

(From behind [Human] Nature, Narcissus, resplendently clothed,
enters as one resurrected. She turns to look at Him.)

*Narcissus*

Shepherdess, why do you weep?
The pearls that you have shed
soften my obdurate heart           1860
and move my soul to pity.

*Human Nature*

I weep for my Narcissus, Sir;
if you have Him, please
tell me where He is,
that I may seek Him out.

*Narcissus*

If nothing can surpass
my own transcendent beauty,
how is it, my dear spouse,
you fail to recognize me?

*Human Nature*

Ay, my beloved spouse,           1870
allow me to approach
and joyfully to kiss Your feet!

*Narciso*

A tocarme no llegues,
porque voy con Mi Padre
a Su Trono celeste.

*Naturaleza Humana*

Luego, ¿me dejas sola?
¡Ay, Señor, no me dejes;
que volverá a insidiarme
mi enemiga Serpiente!

---

## Escena XVI

(Salen Eco, la Soberbia, y el Amor Propio.)

*Eco*

Claro está, pues aunque has hecho          1880
tantas finezas por ella,
en dejándola ¿quién duda
que a ser mi despojo vuelva?

*Soberbia*

Pues no viéndote, ella es
de condición tan grosera,
que dejará Tus cariños
y olvidará Tus finezas.

*Amor Propio*

Y yo pondré tales lazos
en sus caminos y sendas,
que no se pueda librar          1890
de volver a quedar presa.

*Eco*

Yo le pondré tales manchas,
que su apreciada belleza
se vuelva a desfigurar
y a desobligarte vuelva.

### Narcissus

Do not draw near and touch Me
since with My Father I now go
unto His heavenly throne.

### Human Nature

Then, Lord, will you abandon me,
to such excruciating pain?
My enemy the serpent will
return to trick me once again!

---

## SCENE 16

(Enter Echo, Pride and Self-Love.)
[They face Grace and Narcissus.]

### Echo

It is clear that though You've done            1880
so many favors for her,
now that You've left her, who can doubt
once more she'll be my victim?

### Pride

Then, without Your presence,
her state is so precarious
that lacking Your caresses
she'll soon forget Your favors.

### Self-Love

I shall put so many
snares into her pathways,
that all she can become            1890
is a prisoner again.

### Echo

And I shall put so many
blemishes upon her
disfiguring her beauty
she'll lose Your love again.

*Gracia*

Eso no, que yo estaré
a su lado, en su defensa;
y estando con ella yo,
no es fácil que tú la venzas.

*Eco*

¿Qué importará, si es tan fácil                    1900
que, frágil, ella te pierda,
y en perdiéndote, es preciso
que vuelva a ponerse fea?

*Narciso*

No importa, que Yo daré,
contra todas tus cautelas,
remedios a sus peligros
y escudos a sus defensas.

*Eco*

¿Qué remedios, ni qué escudos,
si como otra vez Te ofenda,
como es Tu ofensa infinita,                         1910
no podrá satisfacerla?
Pues para una que te hizo,
fue menester que murieras
Tú; y claro está que no es congruo
que todas las veces que ella
vuelva a pecar, a morir
Tú también por ella vuelvas.

*Narciso*

Por eso Mi inmenso Amor
la previno, para esa
fragilidad, de remedios,                            1920
para que volver pudiera,
si cayera, a levantarse.

*Soberbia*

¿Qué remedio habrá, que pueda
restitüirla a Tu gracia?

### Grace

Not so. I'll be beside her,
defending her from harm;
as long as I am with her,
you will not overcome.

### Echo

Who cares? if being fragile,
she easily can lose you,
for then I guarantee
she'll once again be ugly.

### Narcissus

No matter. I shall give her
help against your cunning,
assistance in her danger,
and shields in her defense.

### Echo

What will help or shield her
if she again commits
an infinite transgression
that You could not redress?
The guilt of one such sin,
required that You die,
and it is very clear
that every time she sins,
it isn't likely that
You'll die again for her.

### Narcissus

Knowing her fragility,
My unbounded love foresaw
her need for remedies
to help her rise again
whenever she might fall.

### Pride

What remedy is able
to restore her to Your grace?

1900

1910

1920

*Narciso*

¿Cuál? El de la Penitencia,
y los demás Sacramentos,
que he vinculado en mi Iglesia
por medicinas del Alma.

*Eco*

Cuando éstos bastantes sean,
ella no querrá usar de ellos,                    1930
negligente, si Te ausentas,
porque olvidará Tu amor
en faltando Tu presencia.

*Narciso*

Tampoco eso ha de faltarle,
porque dispuso Mi inmensa
Sabiduría, primero
que fuese Mi Muerte acerba,
un Memorial de Mi Amor,
para que cuando Me fuera,
juntamente Me quedara.                           1940

*Eco*

Aqueso es lo que mi ciencia
no alcanza cómo será.

*Narciso*

Pues para darte más pena,
porque ha de ser el mayor
tormento el que tú lo sepas,
y por manifestación
de Mi sin igual fineza,
¡llega, Gracia, y recopila
en la metáfora misma
que hemos hablado hasta aquí,                    1950
Mi Historia!

*Gracia*

            Que Te obedezca
será preciso; y así,
escuchadme.

### Narcissus

Which one? She will have Penance
and other sacraments
established in my Church
as healing for the soul.

### Echo

Though these may be enough,
she will neglect to use them;                    1930
if You absent Yourself
she will forget Your love
as soon as You are gone.

### Narcissus

She need not be without Me,
because, from the beginning,
My infinite Wisdom willed
My bitter death become
a remembrance of My love,
so that when I am absent,
I can as well be present.                         1940

### Echo

That is too great a mystery
to be understood by me.

### Narcissus

Then, I shall add to your distress,
because the showing forth
of My unequalled gift
seems to be the greatest
torment that you know.
Come, Grace, and reconstruct
in the same metaphor
that you have used till now,                       1950
my story!

### Grace

It is right and just
that I comply, and so,
hear me.

*Eco*

Ya mis penas
te atienden, a mi pesar.

*Gracia*

Pues pasó desta manera:
     Érase aquella belleza
del soberano Narciso,
gozando felicidades
en la gloria de Sí mismo,
pues en Sí mismo tenía                    1960
todos los bienes consigo:
     Rey de toda la hermosura,
de la perfección Archivo,
Esfera de los milagros,
y Centro de los prodigios.
     De Sus altas glorias eran
esos Orbes cristalinos
Coronistas, escribiendo
con las plumas de sus giros.
     Anuncio era de Sus obras            1970
el firmamento lucido,
y el respandor Lo alababa
de los Astros matutinos:
     Le aclamaba el Fuego en llamas,
el Mar con penachos rizos,
la Tierra en labios de rosas
y el Aire en ecos de silbos.
     Centella de Su Beldad
se ostentaba el Sol lucido,
y de Sus luces los Astros             1980
eran brillantes mendigos.
     Cóncavos espejos eran
de Su resplandor divino,
en bruñidas superficies,
los Once claros Zafiros.
     Dibujo de Su luz eran
con primoroso artificio
el orden de los Planetas,
el concierto de los Signos.
     Por imitar Su Belleza,               1990
con cuidadosos aliños,

*Echo*

Unfortunately, pain
compels my full attention.

*Grace*

This is how it came to pass:
    Once there was that beautiful
and sovereign Narcissus
enjoying great delights
in the glory of Himself,
for in Him and with Him                     1960
was every blessing held:
    King of every beauty,
archive of perfection,
a world of miracles,
and center of all wonders.
    In His highest heavens
were the crystal spheres,
chroniclers who wrote
the script of their rotations.
    The shining firmament                    1970
declared the works of God,
resplendent morning stars
sang Him their joyful praise.
    Fire in flame acclaimed Him,
waters with their curly crests,
earth on lips of roses,
air with whistling echoes.
    A mere flash of His beauty
was the lucid sun's display;
among His lights, the stars                  1980
were only brilliant beggars.
    The eleven sapphires
in their polished settings
served as concave mirrors
of His gorgeous radiance.
    The order of the planets,
and harmony of spheres
with their skillful artifice
were sketches of His light.
    To imitate His beauty,                   1990
fields, with careful grooming,

se vistió el Campo de flores,
se adornó el Monte de riscos.

Adoraban Su Deidad
con amoroso destino,
desde su gruta la Fiera
y el Ave desde su nido.

El Pez en el seno obscuro
Le daba cultos debidos,
y el Mar para sus ofrendas                    2000
erigió altares de vidrio.

Adoraciones Le daban
devotamente rendidos,
desde la Hierba más baja
al más encumbrado Pino.

Maremagnum Se ostentaba
de perfección, infinito,
de quien todas las bellezas
se derivan como ríos.

En fin, todo lo insensible,                    2010
racional, y sensitivo,
tuvo el sér en Su cuidado
y se perdiera a Su olvido.

Éste, pues, hermoso Asombro,
que entre los prados floridos
Se regalaba en las rosas,
Se apacentaba en los lirios,

de ver el reflejo hermoso
de Su esplendor peregrino,
viendo en el hombre Su imagen,                 2020
Se enamoró de Sí mismo.

Su propia similitud
fue Su amoroso atractivo,
porque sólo Dios, de Dios
pudo ser objeto digno.

Abalanzóse a gozarla;
pero cuando Su cariño
más amoroso buscaba
el imán apetecido,

por impedir envidiosas                         2030
Sus afectos bien nacidos,
se interpusieron osadas
las aguas de sus delitos.

dressed themselves in flowers,
and mountains, with their cliffs.
  Wild beasts in their lairs
and birds in happy nests
with instinctive loving
gave homage to their God.
  Deep within the sea's dark womb
fish gave Him worthy worship,
and as her gift, the ocean                    2000
erected glassy altars.
  From grasses of the lowest kind
to the loftiest of pines
all vegetation rendered
devoted adoration.
  The great sea showed itself
in infinite perfection,
from which all other beauties,
like rivers, find their source.
  Lastly, all the mineral,                     2010
rational and sensate world
had its being in His care
and, lacking it, had none.
  Then He, the lovely wonder
Who in the flow'ring fields,
regaled Himself in roses
and feasted on the iris,
    seeing the reflection
of His exotic splendor
in human imperfection,                         2020
fell in love with her.
  His likeness called from Him
such passionate desire,
for God alone is worthy
God's loving to inspire.
  He ventured to enjoy her;
but when He would possess
the lodestone of His longing
with His amorous caress,
    the waters of her sins,                    2030
with envious arrogance,
intervened, impeding
love's suitable advance.

Y viendo imposible casi
el logro de Sus designios
(porque hasta Dios en el Mundo
no halla amores sin peligro),
　Se determinó a morir
en empeño tan preciso,
para mostrar que es el riesgo　　　　　　2040
el examen de lo fino.
　Apocóse, según Pablo,
y (si es lícito decirlo)
consumióse, al dulce fuego
tiernamente derretido.
　Abatióse, como Amante
al tormento más indigno,
y murió, en fin, del amor
al voluntario suplicio.
　Dió la vida en testimonio　　　　　　　2050
de Su Amor; pero no quiso
que tan gloriosa fineza
se quedase sin testigo;
　y así dispuso dejar
un recuerdo y un aviso,
por memoria de Su Muerte,
y prenda de Su cariño.
　Su disposición fue parto
de Su Saber infinito,
que no se ostenta lo amante　　　　　　2060
sin galas de lo entendido.
　Él mismo quiso quedarse
en blanca Flor convertido,
porque no diera la ausencia
a la tibieza motivo;
　que no es mucho que hoy florezca,
pues antes en Sus escritos
Se llama Flor de los Campos,
y de los Collados Lirio.
　Cándido disfraz, es velo　　　　　　　2070
de Sus amantes designios,
incógnito a la grosera
cognición de los sentidos.
　Oculto quiso quedarse
entre cándidos armiños,

(In this world, even God
finds no love without peril);
seeing little or no chance
to succeed in His plans,
    He decided to die
as a pledge of affection,
demonstrating the risk                          2040
of pursuing perfection.
    Paul writes He made Himself lowly,
and, in sweet fire, one might say
that He consumed Himself,
tenderly melting away.
    Like a lover, He descended
to humiliating pain,
and in the end, for love, He went
willingly to death's domain.
    He gave his life to testify                 2050
to the love that He had shown,
but He wished this glorious gift
be not hidden nor unknown;
    a remembrance of His death,
thus He left behind
a pledge of His affection,
a memorial and sign.
    His provision was the child
of His wisdom infinite,
for love shines most resplendent              2060
when understanding glows within it.
    He chose to stay behind,
transformed to a white flower,
for absence might make tepid
the warmth of love's sweet bower;
    no wonder that He blooms today,
already called in Scripture,
the flower of the fields
and lily of the hillocks.
    This white disguise, the veil             2070
of His loving intuition,
cannot be understood
by rude sensual cognition.
    Among the white ermines,
He wished to be concealed,

por asistir como Amante
y celar como Registro:
    que como Esposo del Alma,
receloso de desvíos,
la espía por las ventanas,                          2080
la acecha por los resquicios.
    Quedó a hacer nuevos favores,
porque, liberal, no quiso
acordar una fineza
sin hacer un beneficio.
    Ostentó lo enamorado
con amantes desperdicios,
e hizo todo cuanto pudo
El que pudo cuanto quiso.
    Quedó en Manjar a las almas,                    2090
liberalmente benigno,
alimento para el justo,
veneno para el indigno.

(Aparece el Carro de la Fuente; y junto a ella, un Cáliz con una
Hostia encima.)

    Mirad, de la clara Fuente
en el margen cristalino,
la bella Cándida Flor
de quien el Amante dijo:

### Narciso

Éste es Mi Cuerpo y Mi Sangre
que entregué a tantos martirios
por vosotros. En memoria                            2100
de Mi Muerte, repetidlo.

### Naturaleza Humana

A tan no vista fineza,
a tan sin igual cariño,
toda el alma se deshace,
todo el pecho enternecido
gozosas lágrimas vierte.

### Eco

Y yo, ¡ay de mí!, que Lo he visto,
enmudezca, viva sólo
al dolor, muerta al alivio.

attentive like a lover,
like a bookmark, unrevealed:
    as the spouse of the soul,
afraid that she might fall,
He spies on her through windows          2080
and fissures in the wall.

    He stayed to give new gifts,
because His generosity
demanded He not grant a favor
unless another come to be.

    He showed her His devotion
with prodigal profusion,
and He did all He could
Who could do all He wished.

    He became the food for souls,          2090
No kindness did He spare—
nourishment for the devout,
poison for the unprepared.

(A float with the fountain appears and next to it, a chalice with a
host suspended above it.)

    See, at the crystal rim
of the clear, bright fountain
the beautiful white flower
of which the lover said:

### Narcissus

This is My Body and My Blood,
which I sacrificed for you
through many martyrdoms. Do this          2100
in remembrance of my death.

### Human Nature

Presented with so great a gift,
of unsurpassed affection,
my soul entirely dissolves,
my heart melts with compassion
and pours out joyful tears.

### Echo

Ay, misery! that I have seen Him!
Now silence, claim me; only to grief
am I alive, dead to relief.

### Amor Propio

Yo, absorto, rabioso y ciego,                    2110
venenoso áspid nocivo,
a mí propio me dé muerte.

### Soberbia

Yo que de tus precipicios
fui causa, segunda vez
me sepulte en el abismo.

### Gracia

Y yo, que el impedimento
quitado y deshecho miro
de la culpa, que por tanto
tiempo pudo dividirnos,
Naturaleza dichosa,                             2120
te admito a los brazos míos.
¡Llega, pues, que eternas paces
quiero celebrar contigo;
¡no temas, llega a mis brazos!

### Naturaleza Humana

¡Con el alma los recibo!
Mas el llegar temerosa
es respeto en mí preciso,
pues a tanto Sacramento,
a Misterio tan Divino,
es muy justo que el amor                        2130
llegue de temor vestido.

(Abrázanse las dos.)

### Gracia

¿Pues ya qué falta a tus dichas?

### Naturaleza Humana

Sólo falta que, rendidos,
las debidas gracias demos;
y así, en concertados himnos
Sus alabanzas cantad,
diciendo todos conmigo:

### Self-Love

I, self-absorbed, rabid, and blind,          2110
dangerous, poisonous snake
will die by the poison that I take.

### Pride

I, who caused your fall from grace,
a second time must suffer this:
to be interred in the abyss.

### Grace

And I see that obstacle,
which was your guilt and had so long
been able to divide us,
has been removed and is quite gone;
now, happy Human Nature,          2120
I welcome you into my arms.
Come, then, I wish to celebrate
eternal amity with you;
fear not to come and be embraced!

### Human Nature

With all my soul, I do receive you!
But be aware my hesitation
is only due respect in me,
because to such a sacrament
and so divine a mystery
it is appropriate that love          2130
approach enrobed in holy fear.

(The two embrace.)

### Grace

What does your happiness lack now?

### Human Nature

Naught remains except that we
humbly give our proper thanks;
therefore, let us sing His praises,
chanting hymns in harmony,
each one singing out with me:

(Cantan)

¡Canta, lengua, del Cuerpo glorioso
el alto Misterio, que por precio digno
del Mundo Se nos dió, siendo Fruto                    2140
Real, generoso, del Vientre más limpio!
    Veneremos tan gran Sacramento,
y al Nuevo Misterio cedan los Antiguos,
supliendo de la Fe los afectos
todos los defectos que hay en los sentidos.
    ¡Gloria, honra, bendición y alabanza,
grandeza y virtud al Padre y al Hijo
se dé; y al Amor, que de Ambos procede,
igual alabanza Le demos rendidos!

(They sing)

> Sing, my tongue, the glorious body
> giv'n to ransom the whole world,
> lofty mystery, royal fruit                           2140
> born nobly of the most pure womb.
>     Come, worship this great sacrament,
> replacing ancient sacrifice,
> and all the defects of the senses
> with remedies of faithful love.
>     Glory, honor, blessing, grandeur,
> strength, and laud in equal measure
> be to the Father, Son, and Love
> proceeding from them both. Give praise!

# Notes

## Frontispiece

This portrait has been attributed to Miguel Cabrera, a Zapotec Indian born in Oaxaca, who worked in convents in the capital city and in other cities of New Spain. His works were known to be original and also copies of "trans-Atlantic" well-known works, which he altered to suit his own taste (Robert H. Lamborn, *Mexican Painting and Painters.* New York: 1891). Lamborn believes that Cabrera copied a lost original which was a self-portrait by Sor Juana (13). He purchased the work and later presented it, with others, to the Philadelphia Museum of Art, and it is now part of the Museum's Lamborn Collection.

## The *Loa*

Developed in sixteenth-century Spain, the *loa* generally prefaced a longer comedy or religious play. Whether a *loa* consisted of a few lines, an anecdote, or a short play in itself, *loas* were used, according to Melveena McKendrick:

> to settle the audience, to put it in a good mood, to ask for silence, to grind favourite axes, to attack the *comedia's* detractors, to talk about the actors or other troupes, to explain the work to come when they preceded religious *autos* or to stress the illusionist nature of theater. (139)

Lee A. Daniel details the form's later development by Calderón de la Barca and Sor Juana into a one-act play, "consisting of several scenes, various richly costumed characters, interesting baroque structures and music either as a character or provided by antiphonal choirs" (6). (A parallel development in English drama is the induction. The Christopher Sly plot that prefaces Shakespeare's *The Taming of the Shrew* is perhaps the most easily accessible example that fulfills many of the functions which McKendrick describes.) Although it employs many of Calderón's techniques, Sor Juana's *loa* preceding *The Divine Narcissus* is particularly American in its depiction of Aztecs and its reflection on the problems colonization generated for the Native environment, religion, and population.

## Scene 1

SD *mantas*—panchos; *huipiles*—Aztec women's garment, similar to a pancho, but connected at the sides; *tocotín*—Aztec song and dance.

1–14. Méndez Plancarte summarizes the Mexican creation myth that the sun pierced the earth with an arrow, and from the opening came forth first a man, and then a woman. Huitzilopochtli, the titular deity of the Aztecs, originally thought of chiefly as a god of war, "probably as a result of a process of religious syncretism . . . became identified with the sun (*Native Mesoamerican Spirituality* 191n), and it is he who is called "the god of the seeds."

19–42. The ritual described by Music, America, and Occident of forming the idol from the blood of human victims and seeds, breaking it, and eating it in small pieces parallels the Catholic Eucharistic service closely, but Sor Juana's revulsion toward the Aztec use of human sacrifice is evident in the gory details of Occident's speech, 29–37. As noted by Méndez Plancarte, Sor Juana takes the Aztec ritual from Juan de Torquemada's *Monarquía Indiana*, which speaks of the blood of children. (For hymns and ritual used in child-sacrifice to Tlaloc, god of rain, see *Native* 193–96.)

52–58. As Margaret Sayers Peden suggests, these lines make Sor Juana the first environmentalist in the Americas (*Sor Juana Inés de la Cruz: Poems* 135n).

## Scenes 2 and 3

Méndez Plancarte argues for Sor Juana's essentially orthodox position in relation to the "just war" theory expounded by Thomas Aquinas in the *Summa Theologica*. Accordingly, Zeal's characterization of himself as the scourge of God to punish the sins of the Aztecs and defend the victims of their human sacrificial rites would have to be taken at face value. Religion, however, is notably absent from the military parley, and although in Scene 3, she does not refuse the advantages offered by military action, she puts Zeal in his place as useful only in preparing the ground for verbal persuasion, the *raison d'être* of the *auto sacramental* which she will write through Sor Juana. (Sor Juana's assertions that she herself writes only with her Catholic Religion's permission is ironically reflected in ll, 449–52, and echoes only two years later in *The Answer*.) It is significant that Sor Juana gives to America the most stirring lines in the *loa* (ll. 226–36), which assert the powerlessness of both military and verbal force to subdue her freedom to worship her own gods. It is difficult, even in the face of the Aztec conversion, not to conclude that, however orthodox her beliefs, Sor Juana shows more sympathy in these scenes with the Aztecs than with the representatives of the *conquistadores* and the missionaries. (For an autobiographical interpretation of America's speech, see Arenal, "Aria of a Cloistered Feminist," 52.)

## Scenes 4 and 5

Octavio Paz believes that Sor Juana's emphasis on the parallels between Aztec and Roman Catholic rituals is influenced by Jesuit syncretism, especially as it is expressed by Athanasius Kircher (Paz 350), but as Paz earlier points out (34–43), and the *loa* illustrates, that missionary viewpoint brings about the destruction of native culture. The character Religion's view is less syncretic and more acerbic—that the Aztec religion is only a diabolic parody of the Christian rite. In the *auto*, Satan appears as Echo, a diabolic parody of Ovid's Echo. Are we to assume, then, that Sor Juana agrees with Religion? It is important to remember that the author is not only a nun but a *criolla*, a Mexican-born woman who knows native peoples well enough to depict blacks and Indians in her liturgical plays where native songs, dances, and Nahuatl, the Aztec language are included (Tavard 25). In the final scene of the *loa*, she turns the Jesuit view around 180 degrees by having all the characters sing the glory of God as "the great God of the Seeds," not as Jesus Christ. Although this conclusion has been baptized by citing St. Paul's precedent of identifying Jesus as "the Unknown God" of the Athenians, and the *auto* that follows is a moving affirmation of the loving presence of Jesus in the Eucharist, the baptism of the Aztecs does not take place in the drama. Unlike the historical record, Sor Juana's play leaves them with the right to name their God, and the naming of Christian theological figures and concepts with the language of Greek myth in the *auto* continues to affirm that cultural right. (On allegory as a cultural bridge, see Dinko Cvitanovic, especially 106.)

It is worth pointing out that although Religion recognizes the need to bridge cultural differences with the language of the senses, and historically, *autos* were used to educate the masses, Sor Juana makes clear that her *auto* was meant to be presented at court, perhaps to educate royalty about the treatment of native peoples (see Tavard 25–26). That America's last speech seems to make her a co-author with Religion of the *auto*, appearing at court to make the conventional apology for the work, would support such an interpretation. The play was probably written during 1688, a time of growing political unrest in Mexico, and may have been requested by Vicereine María Luisa, the marchioness de la Laguna, a close friend of Sor Juana and one who carried her work to Spain. Since María Luisa and her husband occupied the governor's palace in Mexico City from 1680 to 1686, she had extensive experience with the difficulties of governing a multiracial colonial province.

# The Auto Sacramental

## Scenes 1 and 2

With its two alternating choruses and leaders, the reader might imagine the opening staged much as the beginning of an opera. Many of Sor Juana's theatrical pieces did have musical settings incorporated with the dramatic texts. However, it is even more likely that the two choruses and leaders alternating verses (taken mainly from the psalms in the case of Synagogue and Ovidian myth in the case of Gentile) were inspired by the Sisters' chanting of the office, which alternates between two choirs with cantors taking some of the verses. For references to particular biblical passages used in the *auto*, see Appendix 1. Synagogue represents the substance of the First Testament, the Jewish Scriptures, while Gentile represents the non-Jewish world, particularly that of the Greek and Roman classics. By providing the Narcissus story, they furnish the allegorical context for the Judeo-Christian story of the Fall and redemption of Human Nature by Christ, which first requires the agency of the fountain, or Mary the Mother of Jesus. Human Nature is not only an allegorical figure but still another female fictional author. She will combine form and substance for the revised Narcissus story. She, in turn, is a creation of Religion and possibly America, who both take responsibility for the *auto* in the apology at the end of the *loa*. And, of course, Sor Juana, the author of all three female authors, seems to be engaging in a self-reflexive exploration of female author-ity in the seventeenth century.

## Scenes 3 and 4

Here begins the Narcissus story revised by Human Nature. "Echo" only appears to be a nymph. It is really Satan who speaks. His friends are Self-Love and Pride. He it is who has the "infused intelligence" characteristic of angels, in this case, a fallen angel. Since he cannot create a new story of his own, he decides to steal the role of Echo in Human Nature's Narcissus/Christ story in hopes of corrupting Human Nature's creation from within. This is exactly what he had attempted with God's creation by tempting Eve after He had been ejected from heaven for disobedience. That story he tells to Self-Love and Pride in this scene. Finally, he continues narrating First Testament history in the form of the *auto sacramental* acted on carts, just as was done in the streets of Madrid in the sixteenth and seventeenth centuries, once again, a self-reflexive device so appropriate for a play about echoes and reflections.

l. 473 Aquarias—aqua=water; the flood that destroyed the world but from which Noah was preserved in the ark; l. 539 Abel—a shepherd killed by his brother Cain, whose son Enoch, who was as good as his father, the first murderer of the Bible, was evil; l.552 Abraham—the patriarch commanded by God to sacrifice his son Isaac. As Abraham drew the knife, an angel intervened and a lamb was substituted for the child. Both Abel and Isaac are considered "types," prophetically prefiguring Jesus Christ.

## Scenes 5, 6, and 7

The activities of Echo/Satan and Human Nature are contrasted in Scenes 5 and 6. In the first, Sor Juana conflates the Ovidian pastoral myth with Jesus' forty days in the desert to fast and pray. There he was tested by Satan, and the forces of good and of evil engaged in the power struggle that would continue until the redemption was completed in the death and resurrection of Christ. Matthew's version is the basis for Sor Juana's amplification of two of the three temptations found in that Gospel. These she imagines taking place on the mountain, a setting more appropriate for the shepherd figure of Narcissus/Christ.

At the same time Human Nature searches for Narcissus, and from l.850, expresses her longing for him in the words of the Canticle of Canticles (Song of Songs), upon which St. Teresa of Avila wrote a commentary and which was used also by St. John of the Cross in his mystical writing. Here Sor Juana gives to Human Nature the passages that describe the Bridegroom. L. 859 Ophir—a country of uncertain location from which gold and jewels were brought to Solomon. In context, Ophir's curls are jewellike or, more probably, golden locks. The description is followed by allusions to several rather obscure prophecies along with those of Isaiah: l. 887 Daniel's vision—a prophetic warning given by God to Daniel that from the decree to rebuild Jerusalem until the Messiah there would be "seven weeks and sixty-two weeks" for the rebuilding of the temple and its consecration; ll. 892–915 Isaiah's prophecies of the birth of the Savior; later, at l. 1,037, "Mordecai's prophetic dream" of a fountain, which Mordecai interpreted as a symbol for his adopted daughter— Esther, X, 5–6, but with which Sor Juana points toward the Mary-fountain in Scene 7. (This is an apocryphal passage, which was part of the Greek Septuagint, and which Sor Juana probably read in the Vulgate.) Esther is a First Testament heroine whose courage saved Israel just as Mary's courageous *fiat* to the Angel Gabriel provides the way to salvation through Jesus. Both Mary and Esther are frequent subjects of paintings by women in the Renaissance and baroque periods. Achaz—King of Judah in the time of Isaiah, who told Achaz to ask God for a sign. Achaz refused, but God gave him one anyway, what has been interpreted as a prediction of the birth of Christ: "Behold a virgin (some translate "woman") will be with child and bear a son, and she will call His name Immanuel." Line 898 "Jesse's mystic root" (Isaiah 11:10)—Jesse is the father of David. Isaiah predicts that Jesus will be born as a descendant of David and Jesse, who is the root of that family tree. Undoubtedly, references to the prophecies help to identify Narcissus with the longed-for redeemer. However, like scholarly footnotes in a love letter, several of these biblical allusions interrupt Human Nature's ecstatic lovesong phrased in the sublime poetry of The Canticle of Canticles. They might all have been more usefully grouped together in Scene 7, which is mainly doctrinal as Human Nature is restored to her former beauty by means of Grace and the fountain who is Mary, the way to Narcissus/ Christ.

## Scene 8

Approaching the fountain also, Narcissus appears as the Good Shepherd described in John 10 and as He who, in Matthew 18 and Luke 15, leaves the ninety-nine sheep to find the one that is lost. The tender tone of the first sixty lines becomes harsh as He details the sins and just punishments due Human Nature/Israel for her unfaithfulness. Here the biblical references are from the First Testament, chiefly Deuteronomy, but the reference to God's feeding Israel with the "choicest wheat" and "fragrant grapes" definitely anticipates the Second Testament Eucharist the play celebrates. At l. 1,227, Narcissus' tone changes abruptly again to that of the Divine Lover who thirsts for souls to return His love. The image of burning thirst anticipates Narcissus'/Christ's thirst as He is dying.

## Scene 9

Sor Juana's stage direction makes no sense. Surely Narcissus does not speak until he arrives at the fountain and gazes at it. Then he addresses the first two ten-line stanzas to praising the fountain itself, which is Mary. Only after these lines does he lean over the fountain and begin the verses of the Canticle of Canticles in which the Bridegroom describes the Bride, who is not Mary, His mother, but Human Nature, whom he sees in His own reflection. In terms of practical stage business, Human Nature should move to the fountain as Narcissus leans over and gazes into it. L. 1297, "Tear away your veil's sheer"—Méndez Plancarte interprets this speech as addressed to the fountain, but the bridal imagery of removing the veil and the direct address to the "spouse" more logically belongs to Human Nature than to Christ's mother. L. 1,301 "Come from Lebanon, the chosen." The adjective seems to modify Lebanon, from which Solomon imported the best and most fragrant woods (cedar and cypress) for building his temple and palace; l. 1,305 Amana, Hermon, and Sanir, "the fragrant diadem"—a crown of mountains in the area of Lebanon and Syria. The cluster of olfactory images related to the geographical area seems to fit together.

## Scenes 10, 11, and 12

This sequence dramatizes the effects of Narcissus' falling in love with His reflection, Human Nature, in the fountain, which is Sor Juana's theological metaphor for the vulnerability of Christ when He takes human nature to Himself in the incarnation. It also poignantly presents Echo's response to Scene 9. Scene 10 presents the result from Ovid, Echo's muteness tied to the biblical account of Narcissus'/Christ's commanding Satan to silence. The earliest example is in Mark 1:23–27. There, Jesus approaches a man "with an unclean spirit" to exorcise him, but first He roughly commands the spirit to "shut up!" as one literal version translates the Greek. In the next two scenes Sor Juana demonstrates her proficiency with the use of the echo in verse with an intricate rhyme scheme and even a pun on the name of Echo. Other, sometimes simpler versions were used by many contemporary writers in both Spanish and English. The echo scene in John Webster's tragedy *The Duchess of Malfi* comes easily to mind. The scene concludes with the Narcissus death speech in the form of a sonnet, in which Sor Juana wonderfully combines the language of the pastoral lover with that of the Gospels.

## Scenes 13 to end

The convulsions in Nature at the death of Christ recorded in the Gospels are narrated first by Echo, Self-Love, and Pride, who attest to the supernatural nature of the phenomena. At least twice in the scene, Echo seems to be echo-ing her author; in ll. 1,633–52, Echo gives a long, highly detailed scientific explanation of the usual causes of an eclipse, which in the last three lines, concludes poetically, just what we might expect to hear from Sor Juana, whose scientific instruments and writing desk were important furnishings in her cell. Later, in l. 1,695, she laments that Narcissus "could thus achieve the great finesse." I translated *fineza* with the root word in order to catch the double meaning of gift and Narcissus' subtle outwitting of Satan by redeeming Human Nature through His death. That is the word Sor Juana used when writing her argument against Vierya and defending St. Augustine's opinion that Christ's greatest gift was to die for humankind. Seeing themselves defeated this time, the diabolic Echo and her side-kicks then plot the further corruption of Human Nature now that Narcissus has died. In the following scene Human Nature mourns the death of Narcissus in the pastoral mode in a duet with Music, who picks up the refrain "Mourn, oh mourn His death!" The verses also mention the scriptural signs of the rending of the temple veil and opening of the sepulchers. Human nature concludes that the entire universe is in mourning and spreads black baize, or funeral cloth, to show its distress, "which extends her grief to the ends of time and space." Then Music and Human Nature go about seeking Narcissus' body, much as Mary Magdalen did on Easter Sunday morning when she found the tomb empty. Grace appears to take the part of the Easter angel who announces the resurrection: "Your Narcissus lives . . . eternally," and Narcissus appears, exactly as Christ appeared to Magdalen, who did not at first recognize Him, to tell her not to touch Him since He must ascend to the Father. Human Nature, of course, feels abandoned. Echo, Pride, and Self-Love hope that she is, but they find that they have been foiled again by the sacramental help Narcissus will give, especially his presence in the Eucharist. But before this final gift is revealed, Narcissus asks Grace to tell his story, continuing to do so in the same metaphor. What follows is a poetic summary of the Gospel in the images of classic myth. Only at the end does the flower that Narcissus becomes turn into the host and chalice of the Holy Eucharist. The play concludes with the hymn of St. Thomas Aquinas to the Eucharist, the *Pange Lingua*, which was traditionally used in Corpus Christi processions throughout Christendom.

# Appendix 1
## Biblical References in
## The Divine Narcissus

RENÉE DOMEIER, O.S.B.

All References are to *The New American Bible,* Trans. Catholic Biblical Association, New York: P. J. Kenedy and Sons, 1970.

### Scene 1

| | | |
|---|---|---|
| lines 1–8 | Psalm 117 | |
| | Psalm 149 | |
| lines 125–26 | Acts 17:28 | St. Paul, in his speech on the Areopagus, cites some of the Greek poets. |

### Scene 2

| | | |
|---|---|---|
| lines 160–92 | Daniel 3:52–90 | Paraphrase of the Canticle of the three youths. |
| | Psalm 148 line 207 | |
| line 207 | 1 Kings 15:19 | Worthiness before the presence of the Lord. . . or in His eyes. |
| | Isaiah 1:16 | |
| | Esther 7:3 line 213 | |
| line 213 | Intercessors: | The good angels and saints of the First Testament. |
| lines 227–41 | Psalm 69 | |
| | Psalm 18:17 | |
| | Psalm 32:6 | |

### Scene 3

| | | |
|---|---|---|
| lines 345–50 | Apocalypse 9:1 | The disobedient angels. |
| | 8:12 | The effect of sin. |
| lines 374–93 | | The angels who have become devils because of pride. They do not lose their gifts of power, knowledge etc. |

| | Isaiah 14:12–20 | As applied literally to the King of Babylonia, though metaphorically to the fall of the Prince of Light, Son of Dawn: Lucifer. |
| | Ezekiel 28:2–19 | As applied to the fallen angels and their punishment. |
| lines 397–400 | 2 Peter 2:4 | They were left with no hope or possibility of repentance. |
| | Judges 6 | |
| lines 473–87 | Genesis 6–8 | The deluge and the salvation through Noah's ark, the "plank after shipwreck." |
| lines 496–503 | Genesis 10:4–9 | Tower of Babel. |
| lines 524–27 | Psalm 113:4–8 | Statues/idols have mouths, but cannot speak. |
| | Psalm 134:15–18 | |

## Scene 4

| lines 536–43 | Hebrews 11:4 | By faith, Abel . . . |
| | Genesis 4:4 | |
| lines 544–51 | Genesis 4:17 | Enoch, the eldest son of Cain, |
| | Genesis 5:19–24 | Enoch, the father of Methuselah, |
| | Genesis 4:26 | Enoch, a grandson of Seth. |
| | Hebrews 11:5 | |
| lines 552–67 | Genesis 22 | Abraham. |
| lines 568–77 | Exodus 32:32 | Moses. |
| lines 584–601 | Isaiah 45:8 | Let the clouds rain down the Just One. |
| lines 646–49 | Isaiah 14:13 | The earthly abode of God. |
| lines 672–85 | Matthew 4:1–3 | Temptation in the desert. |

## Scene 5

| lines 708–819 | Matthew 4:8–11 | Third temptation of Jesus. |

## Scene 6

| | | |
|---|---|---|
| lines 828–30 | John 1:3 | "Through whom all things are made." |
| lines 844–91 | Canticle of Canticles | |
| lines 844–49 | Canticle of Canticles 3:1–2 | |
| lines 850–55 | Canticle of Canticles 5:9 | |
| lines 856–61 | Canticle of Canticles 5:11–13 | |
| lines 862–67 | Canticle of Canticles 5:13–14 | |
| lines 868–73 | Canticle of Canticles 5:15–16 | |
| lines 874–79 | Canticle of Canticles 5:10 | |
| lines 880–85 | Canticle of Canticles 1:6 | |
| lines 886–91 | Daniel 9:24–27 | |
| lines 892–97 | Isaiah 9:6 | |
| lines 898–903 | Isaiah 11:1–3 | |
| lines 904–5 | Jeremiah 23:5 | |
| | Luke 20:41 | |
| | Luke 1:31–33 | |
| lines 905–9 | Isaiah 11:6–7 | |
| lines 910–1004 | Isaiah 11:8–9 | |
| line 916 | Isaiah 7:10–14 | Achaz. |
| line 919 | Jeremiah 31:22 | New thing: a Virgin. |
| lines 922–27 | Genesis 22:18 | |
| | Genesis 26:4 | |
| lines 928–33 | Genesis 49:1,10,18 | |
| line 935 | Isaiah 52:13–15 | |
| | Isaiah 53:1–12 | |
| | Malachi 1:10–11 | |
| line 939 | Jeremiah 29:12–13 | |

## Scene 7

| | | |
|---|---|---|
| lines 1032–5 | Canticle of Canticles 4:12 | |
| | Genesis 2:6 | |
| lines 1037–40 | Esther 10:3 | |

## Scene 8

| | | |
|---|---|---|
| lines 1142–46 | Deuteronomy 32 | Last Canticle of Moses. |
| | Psalm 119:176 | |
| | Isaiah 53:6 | |
| | 1 Peter 2:25 | Lost sheep images. |
| | John 10:14–18 | |
| | Matthew 18:12–14 | |

Luke 15

| lines 1147–51 | Jeremiah 2:13 |
| | Micah 7:16 |
| lines 1152–56 | Deuteronomy 32:6 |
| | John 10:17–18 |
| lines 1157–61 | Canticle of Canticles 5:3 |
| | Matthew 18 |
| | Luke 15 |
| lines 1167–71 | Deuteronomy 32:9–10 |
| lines 1177–81 | Deuteronomy 32:6–7 |
| lines 1192–96 | Psalm 22 |
| | Isaiah 40:11–20 |
| lines 1202–11 | Deuteronomy 32:15–17 |
| lines 1212–31 | Deuteronomy 32:20–25 |
| lines 1232–36 | Deuteronomy 32:39 |

## Scene 9

| lines 1237–41 | John 4:4–7 |
| | John 19:28 |
| lines 1257–77 | Canticle of Canticles 4:2 |
| | Canticle of Canticles 4:3,11 |
| | Canticle of Canticles 5:12 |
| | Canticle of Canticles 7:8 |
| lines 1277–86 | Canticle of Canticles 4:4 |
| | Canticle of Canticles 7:5,7 |
| lines 1287–96 | Canticle of Canticles 4:9 |
| | Canticle of Canticles 5:2 |
| lines 1297–1306 | Canticle of Canticles 2:14 |
| | Canticle of Canticles 4:1,8 |
| | Canticle of Canticles 5:2 |

## Scene 10

| line 1347 | Mark 9:16–24 |
| | Matthew 9:32–33 |
| lines 1358–60 | Mark 1:24–26 |

## Scene 12

| line 1545 | Matthew 26:38 |
| lines 1605–7 | James 4:6 |
| | 1 Peter 5:5 |
| | Proverbs 3:34 |
| line 1616 | John 10:18 |

|                    | Mark 15:37            |
|--------------------|-----------------------|
| line 1621          | John 19:28            |
| lines 1624–26      | Matthew 27:46         |
|                    | John 19:30            |
|                    | Luke 23:46            |
|                    | Psalm 30:6            |

## Scene 13

| lines 1638–43      | Matthew 27:45–53      |
|--------------------|-----------------------|
| line 1671          | Luke 23:47–48         |
| line 1676          | Matthew 27:54         |
| lines 1679–82      | John 12:23–25         |
| lines 1683–86      | John 11:49–52         |

## Scene 14

| lines 1776-79       | Matthew 27:52              |
|---------------------|---------------------------|
| lines 1783–86       | Matthew 27:51             |
| lines 1794–97       | Lamentations 1:12         |
| lines 1798–1801     | Lamentations 1:1–2        |
| lines 1805–8        | Job 16:16                 |
| lines 1809–12       | Psalm 21:15               |
| lines 1816–19       | Canticle of Canticles 8:6 |
| lines 1831–34       | Mark 16:1                 |
| lines 1840–41       | Galatians 2:20            |
| lines 1842–53       | John 20:11–13             |
| lines 1854–57       | Mark 16:6                 |
|                     | Luke 24:5                 |

## Scene 15

| lines 1858–75      | John 20:14–17         |
|--------------------|-----------------------|
| lines 1876–76      | Matthew 28:20         |
|                    | John 14:18            |

## Scene 16

|                    | Luke 22:19                 |
|--------------------|----------------------------|
| lines 1937–40      | 1 Corinthians 11:24–25     |
| lines 1956–2013    | John 1:1                   |
|                    | Psalm 19:2                 |
| line 2017          | Canticle of Canticles 2:16 |
| line 2022–25       | Genesis 1:26               |
| line 2042          | Philippians 2:7            |
| line 2050          | John 15:13                 |
| lines 2067–69      | Canticle of Canticles 2:1  |